CONTENTS

Chapter One: Marriage

Chapter Two: Divorce

Introduction

Marriage and Divorce is the twenty-third volume in the series: **Issues For The Nineties**. The aim of this series is to offer up-to-date information about important issues in our world.

Marriage and Divorce examines current views on marriage and the impact of divorce. The information comes from a wide variety of sources and includes:

Government reports and statistics
Newspaper reports and features
Magazine articles and surveys
Literature from lobby groups
and charitable organisations.

It is hoped that, as you read about the many aspects of the issues explored in this book, you will critically evaluate the information presented. It is important that you decide whether you are being presented with facts or opinions. Does the writer give a biased or an unbiased report? If an opinion is being expressed, do you agree with the writer?

Marriage and Divorce offers a useful starting-point for those who need convenient access to information about the many issues involved. However, it is only a starting-point. At the back of the book is a list of organisations which you may want to contact for further information.

*****

Marriage and Divorce

ISSUES FOR THE NINETIES

Volume 23

Editor

Craig Donnellan

Independence

Educational Publishers

Cambridge

First published by Independence
PO Box 295
Cambridge CB1 3XP

© Craig Donnellan 1996

British Library Cataloguing in Publication Data
Marriage and Divorce – (Issues for the Nineties Series)
I. Donnellan, Craig II. Series
306.8'1

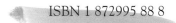

ISBN 1 872995 88 8

Printed in Great Britain
at Leicester Printers Ltd
Leicester, Great Britain

Typeset by
Claire Boyd

Cover
The illustration on the front cover is by
Katherine Fleming / Folio Collective

Family crisis affects us all

Does the rapidly growing number of single parents mean the fabric of our society is being torn apart?

Forget all the politically correct talk that the family is just changing, not declining. We have a historically unprecedented crisis in human relations on our hands.

We have never had divorce rates like this. Now the number of first marriages is lower than it was a century ago when the population was almost half its present size.

These latest figures strike a deathblow to the blasé notion that, while divorce might be booming, marriage is as popular as ever.

But it is not just marriage that is under threat – it is the family.

Marriage creates families, links two sets of relatives and friends and binds men into the long-term care of their children. It is the great cement of society, building connections and creating moral sentiments of commitment and responsibility.

Membership of a family gives individuals a stake in the future, the men a role in life and a place in the community, and children a stable start with two parents for whom their offspring's welfare is their paramount and joint concern.

Without marriage and the family, we lose our links to the rest of the community, our sources of support in adversity and care in old age. These amount to the loss of the framework of society itself.

Marriage is a public statement of commitment and this in turn builds other commitments. It is important for social involvement, personal security, creating role models and providing the moral capital of the next generation.

Despite the scale of the problems involved, the root causes are ignored, denied or seen simply in terms of 'lifestyle choices', women's self-interest or individual happiness.

By Patricia Morgan – Research fellow at the Institute of Economic Affairs and author of Farewell To The Family?

Nobody seems inclined to identify and face developments that are undermining the cohesion of society and its capacity to replace itself adequately. Action is limited to an occasional wince from politicians at the extra 50,000 single parents a year going on the bill for income support.

The most disturbing trend in the decline of marriage is that it leads to the growth of the fatherless society. This in turn means a decline in child welfare and it drives up most social problems such as child abuse, crime, violence and adolescent pregnancies.

A recent investigation of persistent young offenders showed that only a quarter of them live with what were described as two parents and even this included step-parents and mothers' boyfriends.

Four out of five children going into care have lone parents. We know that the death-rate for children under 15 cared for by single mothers on income support is 42 per cent higher than for very poor two-parent and unemployed families.

Surveys of British and American estates also show that the greater the percentage of lone-parent households in the area, the higher the rates of crime and burglary. This is all multiplied when the numbers of broken families and lone parents in an area rises, because it is not just the occasional fatherless family that is a problem, but the rise in the proportion of all families in a community.

It is not just what is lacking in the individual child's home that counts. It is also what happens in the neighbourhood when there is a lack of responsible fathers to supervise youth and enforce standards.

Men not involved with families rarely act as role models and are unlikely to participate in the community . . .from attending a parents' evening at school to trying to improve the local facilities.

Child well-being and success has always depended on the willingness of men to give time and resources to the care of their own offspring. It also gives the men a role.

Being a good father has been seen as the essence of a civilised male. And, since the family-man role is the basis of so many important and valuable habits and attitudes, its absence weakens care and concern in society generally.

Widespread failure of people to marry and rear children means a general collapse of all social continuity and membership.

Marriage and children also provide men with a focus for work effort and commitment. Men are more likely to have and sustain a job when they have some incentive to make an effort – even if that job is dull and hard. As a result, they are more likely to contribute to society rather than being dependent upon it.

The most striking social trend is the sheer increase in men living alone without any family ties or any relationships.

The percentage of males who have never married by the age of 30 has doubled in recent years and now half of all these young males are unmarried.

Events are moving with incredible speed in Britain

Many will be isolated. This in turn leads to increases in crime, suicide, mental and other social problems, and drives up the bill for health, social services, police and prisons.

And, once again, there is a general disintegration in all relationships. While men are more likely to remain unmarried, women are more likely to be unmarried mothers.

Events are moving with incredible speed in Britain. The rate of increase in the unwed birth-rate now outstrips America's, with 32 per cent of all births outside marriage.

That is a rise from one in 20 in 1963, to one in 10 in 1979 and to more than one in three today.

Among births to women under 20, 84 per cent are outside marriage, but other age groups are affected, with one-fifth of births to women over 35 illegitimate compared with one in 10 in 1982.

How can the State possibly take on all the services that marriage provided through mutual support? How can it undo all the disadvantages of children being brought up without fathers and the extended family that marriage provides? And how can it continue to fund the ever-rising costs of the decay of society?

Civilisation is at stake. We have no record of societies without marriage and families.

All societies that have survived have been built on marriage. We can't kid ourselves we are an exception.

Marriage goes on trial as its attraction wanes

Seven in 10 young couples live together for an average of two years before marrying, researchers said yesterday. The number opting for trial marriage before formalising ties has increased 14 times in 25 years.

This suggests that Britain is moving rapidly towards Scandinavian-style 'consensual relationships', said the Office of Population, Censuses and Surveys.

Its *Population Trends* said that the number of first-time marriages had fallen to a level not recorded since 1889 when the population of England and Wales was about half what it is now.

There were 182,000 first-time marriages in 1993, about half the post-war peak of 340,000 in 1972. The total, including second and subsequent marriages, was only 299,000, compared with 426,000 in

By Peter Pallot
Social Services Staff

1972. The last time the number fell below 300,000 (apart from wartime) was in the 1920s depression. Among the findings are:

- The period in which couples cohabit before marriage has increased from one year in the 1970s to two years.
- More than one in five men and women were cohabiting in 1993 compared with one in seven in the mid-1980s.
- Among divorced people, 90 per cent cohabit before marrying again.
- One in four single women is cohabiting – a three fold increase on the 1979 figure.

- One woman in three, often elderly, is now living outside a partnership, compared with one in four in 1979.

John Haskey, author of the analysis, said that Britain was following trends in Sweden and Denmark where most people in their twenties cohabit.

He said there was no sign of a plateau in the decline of marriage. People were deferring marriage later and later and might now never get around to formalising their relationships.

The analysis suggests that the Church of England was doing no more than recognising reality when it said in its 'living in sin' report; that couples often chose to live together after experiencing the divorce of their parents.

Marriage still children's goal

One child in three worries about the possibility of its parents splitting up, with more than a quarter saying couples should stay together even if they are unhappy.

By Flora Hunter

According to a survey of 10-to 17-year-olds published today, most children believe marriage should be for ever and that it is better to live with two parents than one. The *Reader's Digest* MORI poll comes as politicians and sociologists are struggling to come to terms with the changing nature of traditional family values. With right-wing policy makers casting single-parent families, rising divorce rates and the declining popularity of marriage as the root of many evils in modern British society, much has been claimed about the damaging effects on children.

One survey suggests children accept that marriage does not always work. Nearly two-thirds think couples should separate if they are unhappy. While nearly three-quarters said two parents were better than one, 45 per cent did not think it was wrong to have a child outside marriage.

The sixfold increase in the divorce rate in Britain over the past 24 years is reflected in the survey. Most of those questioned knew people whose parents had separated permanently or divorced, split up temporarily or threatened to leave each other.

However, it seems children have not given up on marriage, with 82 per cent saying they were very likely or fairly likely to get married. The preferred age to do so was between 20 and 25.

Reader's Digest editor Russell Twisk said: 'It is heartening to see that marriage still has such strong foundations, and reassuring that our survey shows children holding high ideals.'

Zelda West-Meads, former director of the marriage bureau Relate, agreed. 'This poll shows that the young retain an enormous optimism in the institution of marriage.'

MORI conducted 508 interviews face-to-face among children aged 10-17 in August 1995 at 44 sampling points. © *The Guardian* October, 1995

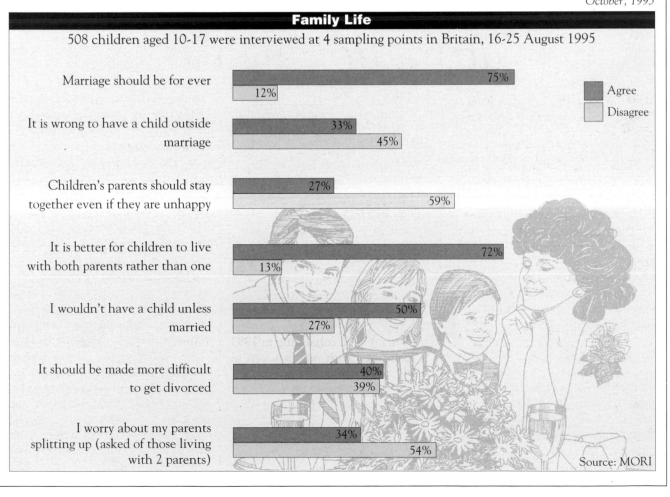

Family Life

508 children aged 10-17 were interviewed at 4 sampling points in Britain, 16-25 August 1995

Legend: ■ Agree □ Disagree

Statement	Agree	Disagree
Marriage should be for ever	75%	12%
It is wrong to have a child outside marriage	33%	45%
Children's parents should stay together even if they are unhappy	27%	59%
It is better for children to live with both parents rather than one	72%	13%
I wouldn't have a child unless married	50%	27%
It should be made more difficult to get divorced	40%	39%
I worry about my parents splitting up (asked of those living with 2 parents)	34%	54%

Source: MORI

Forward to basics

The doomsayers have got it wrong, says Patrick Dixon: marriage and the family are back in fashion

Married couples in future can expect adultery to be a normal part of their lives. Commitment should be based on mutual needs rather than romantic love. Those are the views of Professor Carol Smart of Leeds University, speaking at a conference on marriage in London last week.

Divorced herself, the 46-year-old sociologist said that 'if my partner had an affair tomorrow it would certainly not be the end to everything'. That sort of thing may be fine for her, but 'open marriages' and 'free love' have a disastrous track record, and there is a growing reaction against them.

Despite our sex-obsessed media, the British have always been rather conservative in practice, and are becoming more so. Surveys show that most people are monogamous and most say that adultery is wrong. Romantic love is still very much alive, and so is marriage. Half of all wedding vows last a lifetime and the number of divorces in England and Wales fell in 1994 to 147,080, their lowest level for four years, after peaking at 155,062 in 1993.

These are no freak statistics. It was obvious that the steep rise in divorce rates had to end – or we would all be divorced. From 1971 to 1979 the number of divorces doubled from 75,000 to almost 150,000. However, the figure has since hovered at just over 150,000, with a notable 12-month rise after 'quickie divorce' became law in 1984. The graph has been flattening out for years.

The pessimism over the latest divorce-law proposals, which will overturn 'quickie divorce', is unfounded. The effect of mediation is not yet known but there is no evidence to suggest that the new measures will result in more divorce.

There is now a growing reaction against the excesses of sexual licence, and against the cruel nonsense that more sex must mean more happiness. Just read the agony columns. You can see the changing mood in many parents of teenagers who themselves were products of the 1960s and 1970s. They are against old 1960s values, and lie awake at night worrying about their children's sexual behaviour.

The feelings of parents such as these help explain why the pro-abstinence video *True Love Waits*, produced by the Christian campaigning group the Care Trust, was bought by 60 per cent of all secondary schools last year, while explicit Health Education Authority materials have been falling in popularity. Perhaps that is one reason why the Government has decided to cut the HEA budget from £20 million to £250,000 as from next year. The £19.75 million saved is going to be allocated among competing agencies, including the HEA.

The self-appointed experts on sex education for young teenagers, with their enthusiasm for rolling condoms on bananas, are being marginalised. There are still serious problems, of course. For example, pregnancy rates are high in those leaving school at 16. All the same, young people are far less sexually active than is often supposed. The national sex survey Lady Thatcher tried to ban was finally published last year after 19,000 people had been interviewed. The largest study of its kind ever undertaken in Britain, it showed that three out of four students arriving at university were still virgins. Indeed, virginity is back in style.

What we are witnessing now is a generational shift, brought about in large measure as a reaction against the consequences of permissiveness. We have good reason to be optimistic about the future. But we will not enjoy the fruits of the counter-revolution until we have paid the bill for the sexual licence of the past 30 years. The cost is alarming: some £1 billion just for children in care, of which more than half is related to family break-up, a part of the £9 billion we are paying as individuals or through taxes to help society cope with the results of sexual chaos. That would pay for a quarter of the health service or for 10,000 primary schools.

There is a broken generation of young people as a result of divorce. They have lived through the feuds, the battles, the bitterness. They have friends who have never fully recovered from the isolating numbness, depression and despair. Divorce often means poor exam results, damaged health and stress, four times the risk of needing psychiatric help as a child and a greater risk of breaking down in middle age.

Meanwhile, Aids is modifying behaviour in Europe and the United States, but the figures are still appalling. Aids caused more American deaths last year – just over 50,000 – than the entire Vietnam war. Even if the spread of HIV were halted, the American death-toll from Aids will exceed 15 more Vietnam wars over the next decade. In addition, every 15 seconds someone else in the world is infected with HIV, 20 million so far, mostly heterosexuals, one in 250 of all adults alive today.

No wonder attitudes and behaviour are changing. In spite of all the bad news, though, we remain optimistic about love. Every day almost 500 people in Britain plan a wedding, intending their marriages should last – and the odds are they will.

That is why three out of four polled in an NOP survey last autumn said that divorce should be made more difficult.

'Quickie divorce' reduces marriage to a mere 12-week rolling contract to be together.

There is another factor in the revolt against sexual licence: a restlessness, a deep unease in society, and a hunger for lasting values. We have lived through the collapse of communism and the death of materialistic dreams; we have seen the extinction of idealism and the rise of corruption and sleaze; and the clock is ticking towards a new millennium.

Twelve-year-olds will be waiting to vote as we turn the century. They will reject twentieth-century values as surely as every age has rejected the one before. They will create new architecture, new fashions, new music, new culture, new values, new politics.

There are signs of spiritual renaissance: a grassroots phenomenon, often bypassing traditional sources of spirituality to find meaning, purpose and identity. This week over 40,000 are expected to take to the streets in the latest 'March for Jesus'.

Last June over 10 million people took part in a 'global march' across every time zone, 100,000 in the UK. This is just part of a larger awakening. More people than ever are embracing Christianity, at a rate of 78 million new believers a year – or more than two a second. Islam is also seeing a revival.

The pendulum is now swinging so fast towards 'family values' that politicians are struggling to alter policies quickly enough to follow the public mood. Of course, not everything in the garden is rosy. The daily toll of heartbreak and personal tragedy is far too great to invite complacency, but a change is on the way that could be as significant as any over the past 100 years. There will be no going back to 'Victorian values', but instead a rediscovery that relationships are more important than careers, possessions or free love.
● Dr Patrick Dixon is the author of *The Rising Price of Love* (Hodder, £6.99). © *The Sunday Telegraph plc London, 1995*

Wrangle over cohabitation figures

Challenge to view that married couples stay together longer

By David Brindle

Experts are locked in bitter argument over whether cohabiting couples are much less likely to stay together than those who are married.

The latest research, published in October, suggests that half cohabiting couples split up within three years. By contrast, figures published this week show the average divorce occurs after almost 10 years of marriage. Between a third and half of all marriages are ending in divorce.

The debate was triggered by a claim by Alistair Burt, social security minister, that cohabiting couples were more than four times as likely to split up as those who were married.

Mr Burt cited findings from the *British Household Panel Survey*, which tracks 10,000 people over time. But Mike Murphy, reader in population studies at the London School of Economics, challenged the interpretation and said it was almost certain there was no difference between married and cohabiting couples' propensity to separate if proper allowance was made for the presence of children in a relationship and length of time together.

In October, Nick Buck and John Ermisch, who work on the survey, hit back at Mr Murphy with research showing that cohabiting couples were almost six times as likely to split up as those who were married.

Even where there were children, the researchers said cohabiting couples were more than four times as likely to part. They concluded that 'cohabitation spells are significantly more likely to dissolve than marriages'.

Mr Buck and Mr Ermisch estimate that half of all cohabiting unions end within 32 months – a strikingly similar finding to evidence from the *General Household Survey* that cohabiting couples had been together on average about 32 months.

Studies suggest that about two in three women cohabit in their first partnership. The number of marriages has fallen to the lowest level since the mid-1920s, apart from an artificially low figure in 1943.
© *The Guardian December, 1995*

The decline and rise of the family

Fewer marriages, more divorces and increased single parenting mean that the traditional family is in decline. The family of the 21st century will look very different from today's model

By Catherine Ormell

A house stuffed with smart machines in metropolitan southern England in the year 2050. Inside, a mother in her late fifties gently coaxes her only child away from the 500-channel infotainment system.

An old photograph of a family wedding in the year 1995 has been dislodged by the robot maid. The child's mother, mindful of the world government's slogan 'Learn or Perish', takes the opportunity to teach a little social history. As her seven-year-old strokes his genetically enhanced pet, he asks questions which would sound very strange to us. 'Where are all the old people?' 'Why did granny want to get married?' 'Have I got a father?'

This domestic scene might seem like science fiction to us in 1995 – but it could soon be a reality. The mid-20th-century Western, married, heterosexual, two-parent family living together under one roof is already becoming the exception rather than the norm.

By the end of this century it is estimated that only half of all British children will experience conventional family life with parents who are married at the time of their birth, and who remain married until they are grown up. On current trends, the numbers of lone families, unmarried mothers and cohabitees will continue to grow in Europe and America.

And although the divorce rate may stabilise at its current high level – for every two marriages in Britain in 1991 there was one divorce – marriage looks unlikely to recover its past popularity. It seems the more sophisticated we become, the less likely we are to stay with one partner. The old taboos surrounding divorce and cohabitation have been broken.

It is likely that the family of the mid-21st century will be a pick and mix affair: probably inter-racial, possibly bisexual, certainly multi-generational. Many of its members will be bred using new birth technologies. In the loosely knit clans of 'the blended family', children will have to divide their love and loyalties among different stepmothers, birth mothers, biological fathers and ex-step-parents as well as grandparents.

> **By the end of this century it is estimated that only half of all British children will experience conventional family life with parents who are married at the time of their birth**

New laws will unfold as courts try to settle complex custody disputes. The number of children 'divorcing' their parents will increase – a trend that began America and has already be seen in British courts. Incest could be harder to define.

More pessimistic forecasters warn of the 'daddyless' society where mothers alone bring up children. In Britain the number of lone parents, 90 per cent of whom are women, has doubled in the last 20 years. What's more, our divorce rate is the highest in Europe, and around 50 per cent of children lose contact with a parent – usually the father – two years after the split. Unsurprisingly, studies have found that fathers who don't live with their biological children spend little time with them and offer them little material or emotional assistance.

Women, whether as lone parents or moving through a series of relationships, may become the only stable focus for many youngsters (as indeed they have been for centuries in societies elsewhere in the world). In the next millennium we could see a matrilineal society emerge, where the mother-child relationship is the only indissoluble bond.

So what has happened to the forces that used to bind men and women together into the nuclear families? In Britain the marriage rate has nearly halved between 1971 and 1991, while divorce and cohabitation are on the increase.

Previous generations of women needed marriage for economic support, legitimate sex and social respectability. Today sex is freely available and a single woman – even a single mother on benefit – is a viable economic unit and widely socially acceptable.

The spread of female employment has brought huge changes to domestic life; a new army of cleaners and nannies has been imported into middle-class homes as mothers have abandoned the hearth in favour of the workplace.

Of married and cohabiting British women with pre-school-age children, nearly half are in work today, compared with about a quarter 15 years ago. This trend looks set to continue: during the 1990s women are expected to account for 90 per cent of the net increase in the labour force in Britain.

Penny Mansfield, deputy director of One plus One, a charity which researches marriage and partnerships, believes that marriage – for so long the foundation of Western society – might be replaced by new forms of commitment. 'People will look again at the ways in which they can be committed and this might not be through formal, legal marriage but through something like a joint parental responsibility agreement or a private contract', she says.

If marriage is in decline, then so is reproduction – at least in the West. We're not yet at the stage of needing the state hatcheries of Aldous Huxley's *Brave New World*, but the birth-rate in many European countries has dropped below replacement levels. In Britain the rate is down from 2.4 births per mother in 1970 to 1.8 in 1992; in Italy from 2.4 to 1.3, and even more dramatically in Spain from 2.9 to 1.2 births. In the German state of Brandenburg the local government has taken the unprecedented step of rewarding parents who produce a child with about £416 'child welcome' money in an attempt to reverse the plummeting birth-rate. In America a recent study found that students now rate being well off financially as far more important than raising children.

Next century, the expense of housing, longer periods in education and associated debts will further extend adolescence and postpone parenting. Women are already delaying having children, and having fewer, and this will be encouraged by the reproductive revolution. Donor insemination will become widely available, and infertile women will be able to buy eggs from other women. Women will never have had more choice about when to have a child, and whom to have it with.

John Parsons, consultant in charge of the assisted conception unit at King's College Hospital, London, says: 'I think women will go through the earlier part of their life meeting men and having embryos with them which are then frozen. At an appropriate moment in their careers where they can stop work comfortably, perhaps when they're about 50, they'll thaw the embryos of the men

they decide they really want to have children with.'

Some may take hormone therapy to rejuvenate the uterus and carry a child themselves. Others may hire a surrogate mother or make use of an artificial womb.

Parsons believes that if women have a life expectancy of 100 it makes perfect sense to leave child-bearing until you are 50. 'By the time women get to 50 they will be successful and confident, and make mature decisions about which men to have their embryos with. Also the child will keep the mother young and fit.'

These middle-aged mothers will be part of a trend in the developed world for a society where the old outnumber the young. The Office of Population Censuses and Surveys predicts by 2051 the proportion of people over 75 in the UK will double from 7 per cent to nearly 14 per cent of the population. Children born in 1995 are expected to live to 100.

Much depends on the health of these older people. Pessimists predict a world full of decrepit crumblies, while optimists believe they will all be hale and hearty, with good nutrition, more exercise and medical advances keeping people healthier for longer.

How these elderly fare may have a lot to do with their income and class. The wealthier middle classes have found the family unit a useful mechanism: we look after you in your

---

Women are already delaying having children, and having fewer, and this will be encouraged by the reproductive revolution

---

old age, you leave us your wealth and mind the kids. Further down the social scale, however, where there is no wealth to be passed on and survival is all, the elderly are liable to be dumped by their children. Some geriatrics may have to seek new non-blood relationships – perhaps homesharing like *The Golden Girls*.

The family as a key source of skills and social ideas will change too. Certainly, the traditional invisible hand-down of family skills from generation to generation will not be sufficient preparation for living in 2050. A society nervous about crime and with a huge underclass (jobs will be less secure due to the globalisation of markets) may insist children study the intricacies of human relationships and family management in school and college. New parents will be given effective parenting training and taught how to resolve differences without conflict.

But however these new-style families operate, they will certainly be vastly different from the family as we know it today. Some sociologists believe – or just hope? – that institutions, employers, neighbours and friends will take on roles once dominated by relatives. In the 21st century the blood bond will no longer be one of the strongest links between people.

There will be many more families where non-biological mothers or fathers will be parents, where reproductive technology means the child may not be genetically related – although born – to the mother, and where children have divorced their biological parents and chosen adoptive parents. In the family of the future people will form their own tribes based on choice and affinity, not blood.

Expect the unexpected – 2050
Wild Cards that could upset current trends:

- Resurgence of infectious diseases could decimate elderly populations. Already drug-resistant strains of tuberculosis have been found in several American cities while drug-resistant malaria is rapidly spreading through Asia and Africa.

- Increased male employment. Prospects declined with the switch from a manufacturing to a service economy that favours more part-time jobs and low-paid jobs for women. But increased male employment could make men a more attractive proposition, leading to a revival of the nuclear family.
- Cheaper housing, mass-produced and designed by computer, could slash the current high mortgage burden for families and reverse trends in the West, leading to larger families.
- New studies on divorce and its adverse effects on children may stop couples rushing to split. Equally, research stressing the importance of early mother-and-infant bonding could stem the flow of women back to the workplace after birth.

The family of the future – has *Focus* gone too far?

Is this really what families will be like – an international, multi-racial group, some of whom have shared their genes in ways that the 20th century would consider bizarre? You'll have to wait and see.

Our bet is that some families almost certainly will be just as complex.

But humans – even 21st century humans – are a conservative lot. If you're still around in 2050, you can expect to see a fair number of the conventional, mum-dad-and-2.4 kids kind of family, too.

Why do families exist at all? They provide a means of mutual support, a reef of relationships that protect those inside from the stormy weather of the world. If any kind of extended, high-tech, heterosexual-homosexual multi-everything 'kin group' is to thrive it will have to do the same job as well as more orthodox families.

The fast-changing face of the family in our own time

The ageing population
The number of people in Britain over pensionable age is projected to exceed over 16 million by 2031 – more than twice the number in 1961.

Single parenthood
In 1991 just over 17 per cent of families with dependent children were headed by a lone mother and only one per cent by a lone father.

Marriages
For every two marriages in Britain in 1991 there was one divorce. One in five unmarried men and women aged 16-59 were cohabiting in 1992.

Household size
Since the Second World War the average household has fallen from just over three people in 1961 to 2.5 in 1991.

The darker side of the nuclear family

Marriage rates peaked in the fifties when post-war prosperity enabled many young people to move away from their parents and into their own homes. Pre-marital sex, cohabitation and illegitimacy fell to low levels, helping to foster the illusion of a golden age of family.

The less attractive side of this apparent domestic idyll was that many people were trapped in unhappy marriages, few fathers participated in their children's upbringing, and single women who became pregnant were often ostracised and forced to give their babies up for adoption.

Today, families may be less likely to eat together, but they do shop, eat out in restaurants, and visit leisure centres together.

Next century, expect families to take learning holidays together and even work together. As parents increasingly begin to work from home, so children will help out with computer or administrative tasks – in return for extra pocket money.

Social meltdown

Some in the UK and Britain predict that recent social changes could fracture society irredeemably. In particular they argue that the dramatic increase in absent fathers means vast numbers of children lack a male role model and basic discipline.

More single-parent families and dual-wage-earner families mean that children generally get less attention. A study by the University of Maryland found that parents today spend 40 per cent less time with their children than they did in 1965 – 17 hours a week compared with 30 hours.

The numbers of latchkey children has gone up. Estimates suggest that there are between 9 and 12 million in the US. Some experts argue that children left alone for long stretches of time are more likely to be tempted on to the streets, triggering a crime timebomb.

Some research indicates that children living with single parents or in stepfamilies are more likely to fail in school and require more treatment of emotional and behavioural disorders than those who live with their biological parents.

© *Focus*
January, 1996

Changes in family structure

From Barnardos

- Families have got smaller: the average number of children per woman has declined to 1.8; mothers are getting older: the average age at childbirth has gone up to 28 (England and Wales) (Woodroffe *et al* 1993).

- The divorce rate has increased markedly, and Britain has the highest divorce rate in the EC apart from Denmark (*Social Trends 1993*). The number of persons divorcing per 1000 married people in Britain rose from 4.7 in 1970 to 13.0 in 1990 (*General Household Survey 1991*), and it is estimated that if divorce rates stabilise at their present levels, 37% of marriages will end in divorce. In 1991, 56% of divorcing couples in England and Wales had children under 16 (OPCS Marriage and Divorce Statistics 1991). In that year over 160,000 children experienced the divorce of their parents, and an unknown number of others will have experienced the separation of cohabiting parents. At least one in five children can expect to experience their parents' divorce before they are 16.

- There has been a large rise in the proportion of children whose parents are living together but are not married. Many of these cohabiting couples are in stable long-term unions and are really little different from married couples. However, in comparison with married-couple families, cohabiting-couple families have, on average, lower household incomes; they are more likely to be in receipt of income support and housing benefit, and in local authority accommodation; and the man is more likely to be unemployed or to be in semi-skilled and unskilled occupations (Kiernan and Estaugh 1993).

- A growing proportion of births are occurring outside marriage, especially among young women, but over half of these babies are being born into families headed by a cohabiting couple. The percentage of live births occurring outside marriage has grown from 9% in 1978 to 31% in 1992 in England and Wales (*Population Trends 1993*). Among the live births outside marriage in England and Wales in 1992, 55% were registered jointly by parents with the same address, 21% were registered by two parents with different addresses, and 24% were registered solely by the mother i.e. 8% of all births (but note that babies in the last group could have cohabiting parents with the father not present at registration, owing perhaps to constraints on time or money or simply because of not knowing that attendance would be required for registration). Sole registration is much more common among young women. Among women under 20, 83% of live births were outside marriage in England and Wales in 1991, and 35% of these births were sole registrations (i.e. 29% of all births to women in this age group) (OPCS Birth Statistics 1991).

- There has been a large rise in the proportion of children being brought up in a family headed by a lone parent. In 1991 lone-parent families made up nearly 20% of all families with dependent children, compared with 13% in 1981 and 8% in 1971, and they were caring for about 2.2 million children – 18% of all children living in families. 90% of lone parents are lone mothers. 65% of lone mothers are either separated, divorced or widowed, and 35% are single i.e. never married, though possibly cohabiting when their babies were born (*General Household Survey 1991*, Haskey 1993). The UK has a higher proportion of families headed by a lone parent than any other EC country (Roll 1992), though the UK has not reached the levels of the US, where 25% of families are headed by a lone parent.

- The average duration of lone motherhood is estimated at about five years for previously married lone mothers, and about three years for single (i.e. never married) lone mothers (Ermisch 1992).

- Many children in lone-parent families lose contact with their absent parent. Lone parents report that after two years of lone parenthood about 40% of absent parents are out of contact with their children (Bradshaw and Millar 1991).

- A significant number of children now live in stepfamilies. 8% of families with dependent children contain one or more stepchildren (*General Household Survey 1991*).

References

Bradshaw J and Millar J (1991) *Lone Parent Families in the UK*. HMSO, London.

Ermisch J (1992) *Lone Parenthood: An economic analysis*. Cambridge University Press.

Kiernan K and Estaugh V (1993) *Cohabitation: Extra-marital childbearing and social policy*. Family Policy Studies Centre, London.

Woodroffe C, Glickman M, Barker M, and Power C (1993), *Children, Teenagers and Health: The key data*. Open University Press, Buckingham.

● The above is an extract from *All our futures* by Sally Holtermann, published by Barnardos. See page 39 for address details.

© *Barnardos*

Making a success of marriage

Amid mounting hysteria about the future of marriage, a surprisingly optimistic view of it comes from America's leading expert on divorce. Rosalind Bayley talks to Judith Wallerstein about her new book *The good marriage*

It is a peculiarity of our society that what we know about good things comes from learning about what is bad. Take marriage. When psychologist and expert on divorce Dr Judith Wallerstein started her study of good marriages, she had no psychological theory or clinical categories to rely on because virtually no research has ever been done on successful partnerships.

For this reason she started with a small, handpicked sample of 50 couples, both of whom believed their marriage was happy, and almost all of whom were middle-class Californians.

She accepts that the study is not representative of America in class or ethnic terms. 'When you enter a field and want to build hypotheses, you try to get a reasonably homogeneous group to explore the differences in marriage rather than class and ethnic differences.'

What she found was different forms of marriage that provide different degrees of closeness, different roles and different divisions of labour and responsibility between the husband and wife.

Exploring the dynamics of the different types of relationship, she classified them into romantic, rescue, companionate and traditional marriage.

One of the findings that surprised her was the ability of a good marriage to heal the scars of childhood. Having parents who were happily married was far from a prerequisite for having a good marriage yourself.

A fifth of the couples were in 'rescue' marriages, where the individuals had through their marriages put often extremely traumatic childhoods behind them. Many of the men who formed romantic marriages had had very lonely childhoods and many of the women had had difficult relationships with their own mothers.

Despite years of working with the products of failed marriages – 'I've seen more children of divorce than anyone else in America' – she does not share the doom-and-gloom view that modern marriage is bankrupt, or want a return to 'traditional marriage.'

'The people in these marriages took advantage in a good way of the freedom that society now offers, particularly for the women the freedom that their mothers and grandmothers lacked.'

Significantly, only five of 100 individuals she interviewed wanted a marriage like their parents had. 'Marriage today is a different institution.' Marriage used to be held up from outside, by the church, the law and the extended family. Now it is only held up from within.

'The men and women have to make many more decisions because they are not following traditional routes.' Economic pressures in families make marriage much tougher. 'Marriage is hard. It is under the gun in terms of the workplace.'

Because it is now so much more difficult to succeed, more must be learned about marriage and more done to prepare people for it.

The book is not a manual, and Wallerstein is chary of saying how or when young people should be prepared for marriage. But she is hopeful that her work will give some pointers to the route.

The nine tasks

She identifies nine lessons or tasks that a couple must undertake if they are to make a success of their marriage, including separating from parental families, building intimacy and autonomy, dealing with conflict, preserving romance, nurture and fun, and adjusting to children and change. All hinge on a deep and expressed commitment, not just to each other but to making the marriage work.

This points to an important difference between marriages, and within that she includes cohabiting

relationships undertaken as long-term committed partnerships, and just living together.

'Because they figure that the relationship is not for keeps they don't exercise the same criteria in choosing. The man is cute and good fun. The woman doesn't have to think if he would be a good father or would take care of her if she was ill.'

The two types of relationships will work differently too. 'There are different images and different ghosts that inhabit a marriage.'

She partly blames her own profession – she trained as a psycho-analyst – for misunderstandings about marriage.

'We have totally under-estimated the amount of change that takes place in adulthood and have failed to grasp that the marital relationship is the central axis around which this change takes place.'

This is because psychology has been over-captivated by the importance of childhood.

Her experience of the happy marriages showed not that all the individuals started out with advanced interpersonal skills – 'you don't get to be a hot shot in corporate life in America by being empathetic' – but that there was an expansion of empathy that came through that relationship.

'There are different images and different ghosts that inhabit a marriage'

And she does not duck from the damage that marriage can cause. 'A bad marriage has a tremendous power to destroy, for regression.'

She believes that many of the failed marriages she has seen could have been saved by following the lessons from the successful couples – those that fail because of unemploy-ment, illness, the intrusions of the workplace or under the pressure of the birth of the first child.

Some were probably beyond redemption. 'If you have no capacity to put yourself in another person's shoes, then don't get married.'

The good marriage: how and why love lasts, by Judith S Wallerstein and Sandra Blakeslee, was published by Bantum in the UK in January 1996.

● The above is an extract from *Family Policy Bulletin*, published by the Family Policy Studies Centre. See page 39 for address details.

© Family Policy Studies Centre
November, 1995

Mum's no longer the word for many women

A survey shows that more young women predict they will have no children. But, asks Christina Hardyment, do they mean it?

Who needs children these days? They are just a worry, and there's not much future for them anyway. Besides, they'll clutter up my career.'

The latest scare story from the statisticians is that opinions like this are increasingly common. We are apparently turning into a nation of unfamily-friendly egotists, who decide that the child-free life has a lot more to offer than coping with nappies, nose-wiping, shrinking child allowances and a 10-year sentence of attendance at the PTA.

Women born since the 1960s are twice as likely to remain childless as those born in the 1950s or earlier, according to projections from the Office of Population Censuses and Surveys. This means that as many as a fifth may not have children.

To counter this trend, a report issued yesterday by the Family Policy Studies Centre recommends that policy-makers should now be looking for ways of making family life more attractive.

Nobody glancing at the contents of women's magazines or watching the distinctly unmaternal Saunders and Lumley in *Absolutely Fabulous* would be surprised that more women appear to be turning away from motherhood. *Cosmo, Elle* and *Options* all outline a world of feisty, young professional women for whom a man is as much an optional accessory as a Hermes scarf. Children are merely dots on the distant horizon of their 30th, or even 40th, birthdays. So are we finally getting our comeuppance for three decades of relentlessly pushing an image of femininity in which maternity plays little or no part?

The short answer is no. At least 10 per cent of women have always been childless for one reason or another. Nor, reading the small print of the FPSC report, is there any hard evidence that there is a significant increase in the women who delib-erately choose to remain childless for the sake of their careers, their designer clothes and exotic holidays. What *has* changed is that fewer women are having babies simply because they feel it is expected of them.

'Feminism has given women the courage to come out and say they don't want children; it has legitimised such a choice', says Jane Bartlett, whose book *Will you be Mother? Women who choose to say no* was published last year. Nor did she find any evidence of a new breed of materialistic career women who selfishly wanted to stick to the single

life. 'They actually had a high sense of the value of motherhood: they thought it was something that was too precious to take on unless you could do it well.'

Increasingly perfectionist standards were also pointed to as demoralising. 'You seem to have to give up so much to be a good mother – and, in the eyes of the world, mothers are always in the wrong,' said one nervous interviewee. Others pointed to the practical difficulties of having children and keeping a job: discouraging work environments, expensive child-care and the stresses they could see being imposed on contemporaries who were already mothers.

But such decisions were far from being easy. Some still had regrets, and a sense of loss. Many had to battle with family opinion. One was given a pram as a wedding present by her mother-in-law. 'It gathered mildew in the garage until my husband explained to his mother that he'd had a vasectomy.'

Bartlett feels that although choosing not to have children is now more acceptable, it is only the furthest end of a continuum. Right across Europe, fertility has plummeted – Spain and Italy, Roman Catholic countries traditionally associated with large families, are at the bottom of the child-bearing charts, with an average of only 1.3 children per potential mother.

Having fewer children is deemed wise in economically anxious times, but it is rather different from deliberately deciding to have no children at all. The figures are further distorted by the trend for women to choose to have children later in life.

'You seem to have to give up so much to be a good mother – and, in the eyes of the world, mothers are always in the wrong'

Meanwhile, the women who deferred having children often find themselves involuntarily contributing to the absolute increase in childlessness. The perils of postponement are manifold. Relationships are much less stable now that there is so much of a gap between the age of first intercourse and becoming a parent. Many of the women interviewed by Jane Bartlett did not actually reject the idea of having a child; they just hadn't ever found themselves in a situation which they felt was right for them.

It may be that women are more ambitious to achieve the perfect material and emotional circumstances for parenthood. Certainly, it is widely felt that the mechanics of social introductions are highly unsatisfactory in modern society. Once the first wave of school and university encounters with the other sex passes, the chances of meeting the right father for one's child lessen dramatically.

Or he simply turns up too late. What has happened since the Pill made it so easy to separate passion from procreation is that we have, like sorcerers' apprentices, interfered with the natural course of female fertility without quite knowing where to stop.

A growing number of women over 30 are finding it much harder to have babies when they want to. Fertility declines dramatically with age. Added complications are the inhibitory effect on fertility that staying on the Pill seems to produce, and the decline in male sperm count.

What about the effect of divorce? Are there a growing number who have found the experience of witnessing their own parents' unhappiness traumatic? 'I just didn't want to risk putting children of my own through what I went through,' says Christine Black, now a successful teacher of graphic design.

On the other hand, many looked on parental troubles as a challenge. 'I think it had the opposite effect on me,' says a well-adjusted child of divorce, who has two sons and a thriving career in broadcasting. 'I just decided that I could do a whole lot better.'

What no survey has been able to prove is that childless women are being deliberately selfish. Perhaps we should rather applaud their courage for perceiving that an unwanted child is a social liability.

Family index

Marriage, divorce and cohabitation

By Natalie Cronin

Men and women are marrying later and fewer are marrying, although the majority of people in the UK will marry at some stage and six out of ten are currently married.

The actual number of marriages has been falling steadily over the past 20 years. In 1992, there were 347,000 marriages in Britain, a rate of 12.2 per 1,000 population of all ages. The proportion of first marriages has also declined since the 1970s: only 61% of marriages were between a bachelor and a spinster in 1992, compared with 85% in 1961. A growing proportion of marriages involves remarriage for one or both partners. In 1992, 21% were first marriages for one partner only, compared with 12% in 1971.

The decline in marriage can partly be explained by the sharp increase in age at first marriage over the last two decades. Between 1971 and 1992, the average age at first marriage jumped from 22.6 years to 25.9 years for women and 24.6 years to 27.9 years for men. A number of factors help explain why men and women are marrying later: increased and longer participation in further and higher education, high rates of unemployment among young people and the growing popularity of pre-marital cohabitation.

If present marriage rates continue, then the expected proportions of men and women married by age 50 would be around 77% for men and 78% for women, compared with 93% of women and 96% of men in 1971.

Cohabitation

Alongside the sharp fall in marriage rates since the early 1970s there has been an increase in the proportion of cohabiting couples. General Household Survey data indicate that in 1979, just 3% of all women aged 18-49 and 8% of all single women were cohabiting; by 1993 this had increased almost threefold to 9% and 22% respectively, and 18% for non-married men. The duration of cohabitation, however, has remained virtually unchanged. Amongst never-married women, it increased only slightly from 18 months in 1979 to 21 months in 1989.[1]

Cohabitation varies markedly between age groups. The peak age for women is between 25 and 29 when almost three in ten (28%) non-married women are cohabiting, and between 30 and 34 for non-married men when a third (33%) cohabit. The relatively high proportions of around a quarter cohabiting among 40-44 year-old non-married women and 45-49-year-old non-married men correspond to the rise in post-marital cohabitation amongst that age group.

Living together before marriage has become increasingly common. Just over half (51%) of women marrying for the first time in 1989 had lived with their husbands prior to marriage compared with 19% of those marrying in the late 1970s and only 7% of those marrying in 1971.

Divorce

In 1992, there were 160,000 divorces in England and Wales, a rate of 13.7 per 1,000 married population, or one divorce for every two marriages taking place in 1992. The number of divorces doubled at the beginning of the 1970s, following legislation in 1969 which introduced the irretrievable breakdown of marriage as a ground for divorce. But since the end of the 1970s the rise in divorces has been much more gradual. The peak figure in 1985 reflects further legislative change in 1984. In 1992, one in twenty (4%) of the total adult population were divorced or separated. Since the end of the 1970s the legal process of divorce has been initiated by women in around 70% of cases.

Divorces have been occurring increasingly early on in marriage. Of marriages that took place in 1951, 10% had ended in divorce by the end of 25 years. In contrast 10% of couples who married in 1971 were divorced by their 6th wedding anniversary and 10% of those married in 1981 had divorced within 4.5 years. Estimates suggest that if divorce rates prevailing in the 1980s continue, then just under four in 10 (37%) marriages contracted in the mid-1980s are likely to end in divorce.[2]

Although three out of ten couples who divorce are childless, a growing proportion of children are affected by family breakdown. In 1992, the number of children under 16 with parents who divorced was 169,000. Of these, one-third (32%) were under-fives compared with a quarter (25%) in 1971. This proportion has been increasing as divorce occurs earlier in marriage. If present trends continue, around one in four children will experience the divorce of their parents before they reach 16.[3]

References:
1 *The Family Today*, 1990, FPSC
2 'Current prospects for the proportion of marriages ending in divorce', *Population Trends*, 1989
3 'Children in families broken by divorce', *Population Trends*, 1990

● The above is an extract from the *Family Policy Bulletin*, produced by the Family Policy Studies Centre. See page 39 for address details.
© *Family Policy Studies Centre July, 1995*

A man for all reasons

Arranged marriage versus love match: Yasmin Alibhai-Brown hears two views

Jeyaben Desai, an extraordinary Asian woman who led one of the most prolonged and highly publicised industrial disputes in this country, at the Grunwick photo processing plant in the seventies, once told me her views on marriage: 'You girls have no idea what it means. You watch all this romance on the screens and think that is how you can find a life partner. Marriage is something not between two individuals, but two families, two histories. It is a serious business and you need to be realistic about the choices you make. These Romeos, these instant passions, soon disappear Then comes bitterness and frustration. We married men carefully chosen by our parents; they looked for long-term qualities, like wisdom, responsibility, respect.'

Most of our elders would take a similar view. That we simply fail to understand what is required for a lifelong partnership, that we are captives of men's sweet talk and false promises, that to follow something as unreliable and fragile as our hearts when choosing a husband is foolish and dangerous. In Asian homes across the land, mothers use these arguments to persuade (and sometimes force) their daughters not to abandon tradition.

Asha, whose daughter Nimu has just announced that she is marrying a divorced Englishman, can talk of little else. 'She has just gone off her head. I look around at our girls these days, running away with men they hardly know. Why do you think there is so much divorce? Because they do no research and the men have no sense of obligation. Do you see our men running away with their secretaries? Nimu's father and I started life together knowing little about each other, only a few steps up the mountain, so slowly we could get to the top. Nimu is at the top already, the only place to go is downhill.'

Nimu, a forthright woman in her thirties, is unimpressed. 'You accepted things, you had no choice. We have a choice and we can have the kind of relationship you could not even dream of. You were taught to pretend you were happy, to put yourself last, I will not do that.'

'Marriage is something not between two individuals, but two families, two histories. It is a serious business and you need to be realistic about the choices you make'

I remember similar battles when I was growing up in Uganda in the sixties. Ours was the generation that discovered love, wet kisses, Elvis and Cliff. Heartbreak too. Suddenly the world inhabited by our parents appeared drab and depressing.

Women like my mother did marry for life. Most never discussed their pain, their disappointments or even their joys. I still wonder how many knew sexual pleasure. And yet many were glowingly happy, adored by their men (who were always described in solid terms such as 'dependable'). The art, we were constantly told as girls, was to find ways of keeping the husband content and if anything was going wrong, never to talk about it. But you knew when a woman was unhappy. She was usually the one who prayed most fervently and longest in the mosque, eyes tightly shut, the beads on her rosary rattling past her fingers at furious speed. Sometimes there would be whispers of a suicide, always without a note, discreet to the end.

We lost or willingly gave up that stoicism and patience. We became more demanding, greedy for pleasure, undaunted by shame, personally more fulfilled. Sometimes it was easier to find this with men outside our communities and inter-marriage between Asian women and white men has increased dramatically.

But now something else is also beginning to happen. Those of us who are older and perhaps disillusioned in different ways can see that, although there were many stifled tragedies, when their marriages worked, our elders did create families that were more solid, cohesive and enduring than ours. They were wise, after all. Even more interestingly, many younger Asian women, brought up in Britain, are seeking to recreate that past in their own lives. Call it the new conservatism, the search for roots, the backlash,

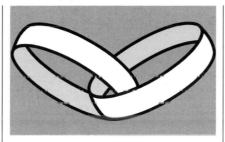

whatever, more and more middle-class professional Asians are asking their parents to arrange their marriages.

Mariyam, a recently graduated doctor, has been pressing her parents to do this for months. The reason, she says, is simple. 'I want the marriage they have. They respect each other. They are partners, not competitors. Never in a million years would they think of breaking up, not even when things have been terrible between them. I look around at all these fickle relationships and I am

scared of ending up in one. Marriage is more than good sex, excitement, even friendship. And our people are better at it than any of the other communities in this country. So why give up something that is working?'

Her mother Suraya will not hear of it. 'You wouldn't survive five minutes. It was different in our time, that was what we grew up to expect. With all this education and freedom you have, how will you comply with the demands of a joint family and a traditional husband? You will fail and then blame us.

'No, go and find a husband, make sure he is a good man and a good Muslim, don't bother us.

'You have so many chances I never had, don't throw them away.'
● *No Place Like Home* by Yasmin Alibhai-Brown is published by Virago at £8.99. © *The Guardian* September, 1995

44 *per cent of pregnancies now occur outside marriage*

By Rebecca Pike

Almost half of all pregnancies in England and Wales occur outside marriage, according to Government figures released yesterday.

The proportion of pregnant women who are unmarried reached 44 per cent in 1992, from 30 per cent 10 years earlier, according to the Office of Censuses and Population Surveys.

While the number of women becoming pregnant in 1992 – about 828,000 – fell by 3 per cent from the previous year, the number becoming pregnant outside marriage rose from 226,590 in 1982 to 364,320 in 1992.

Of these, 34 per cent ended in abortion, compared with 8 per cent of conceptions within marriage.

By contrast, the number of girls conceiving under the age of 16 fell by 7 per cent between 1991 and 1992, from 7,800 to 7,300. The number of women becoming pregnant under the age of 30 also dropped, while the rates for older women rose.

The largest proportionate rise (9 per cent) was for women aged 40 and over.

The figures come only days after it was revealed that the divorce rate was at an all-time high and the popularity of marriage at a 50-year low.

Statistics from the OPCS for 1993 showed that the number of couples divorcing that year reached 165,000, while the number of marriages fell below 300,000.

However, a spokesman for the National Council for One-Parent Families said the figures should be taken in context.

'The vast majority of births outside marriage are registered by both parents, indicating that more people are choosing to have children within a relationship rather than as single parents,' she

said. But the proportion of people having children outside marriage shows there is a need to develop support services for this type of family.

'The figures for girls under 16 contradict the impression often given in the media that the number is going up.'

The highest teenage conception rate among district health authority areas was in north Manchester (128 per 1,000 women aged between 15 and 19), which also had the most conceptions for girls under 16.

South-west Surrey had the lowest teenage conception rate (29.4 per 1,000 women aged between 15 and 19) and the lowest conception rate for women aged 15 to 44 (61.7 per 1,000)

East London and the City had the highest overall conception rate with 117.1 per 1,000.

© *The Telegraph plc* London, 1995

Divorce rate falls after years of relentless rise

By David Fletcher
Health Services
Correspondent

The divorce rate has started to fall for the first time after more than five decades of steady increase, according to preliminary figures for last year.

They show that divorces in 1994 totalled 155,332, a drop of almost 10,000 over the previous year when the number of divorces reached its highest level and the number of marriages was at its lowest.

The slow-down was greeted by Relate, the marriage guidance council, as the first sign of a determination among couples to make their marriages work.

Denise Knowles, spokeswoman for Relate, said: 'It's too early to say we've turned the corner, but this is a great start.'

She said there had been a one per cent increase in the number of interviews – a total of 405,000 – held by Relate counsellors in 1993.

'That's a positive sign because it shows more people are taking their marriage commitment more seriously and seeking help. It could be that couples are waking up to the realisation that broken marriages are tremendously traumatic for their children,' she said.

The drop may be short-lived, however, as a result of the new Divorce Bill to be announced in the Queen's Speech next month. It will enable divorces to be granted after a year in all cases.

Although the Bill will end 'quickie' divorces – which caused divorces to double in a year when they came into effect in 1971 – it will require couples to wait at least a year after starting proceedings before divorcing.

The intention is to provide a year-long period for reflection and mediation while reinforcing the Conservatives' image as the party of the family.

But critics say it will make divorce automatic on the application of one of the partners and send the divorce rate climbing even faster.

Under existing arrangements four marriages out of 10 end in divorce, giving Britain the highest rate in Europe.

John Taylor, the parliamentary secretary to the Lord Chancellor's Office, described last year's decrease as both substantial and encouraging. He is closely involved with a working party set up by the Government to look at the idea of 'marriage lessons'. He said the group would try to identify the needs of couples preparing to marry, find out what existed for them and let them know of the best services available.

'By the end of the process, couples thinking of marriage should be able to tap into a network of literature or counselling around the country. Most importantly they will know what's out there for them.

'I deplore the idea of "marriage lessons" becoming compulsory, but we need to do all we can to make seeking help seem normal and natural rather than freakish and eccentric,' he said.

Figures from the *Office of Population Censuses and Surveys* last August showed that the number of divorces reached an all-time high in 1993 while the number of marriages slumped to its lowest level for 50 years. There were 299,197 marriages in 1993, a fall of 4 per cent, or 12,000, on the previous year. It was the first time since 1943, when the number was affected by war, that fewer than 300,000 couples had married.

The fall in marriages was matched by a fourth consecutive increase in marriage failures, taking the divorce total to 165,018, the highest in history.

© The Telegraph plc London, 1995

Putting off the big day

The death of the institution of marriage has been greatly exaggerated, according to a survey today which shows that couples are postponing, rather than abandoning, the decision to marry.

A Gallup survey, commissioned for ITV's documentary *World in Action*, found people still want to get married, but only when it suits them.

More than half of the unmarried couples questioned – 52 per cent – said they would 'definitely' get married in the future while a further 28 per cent said they probably would.

The most popular reason for getting married was love, more than three-quarters citing it as their reason, while having children was second on the list at 13 per cent.

However, the stigma of having children outside marriage appears to have all but disappeared, with 72 per cent claiming it was socially acceptable.

© The Telegraph plc October, 1995

Divorce became legal in 1857 – and only 24 couples took advantage of the new freedom during the first year. The number has been climbing more or less continually ever since – and the figures show that each change in the law has been followed by a surge in divorces.

There seems little doubt that the proposed Divorce Reform Bill, however well intentioned, would have the same effect. The annual divorce figure was 580 in 1911 and the rate of increase was extremely slow until the first major liberalisation in 1937.

Since then the rise has been dramatic, even without the spectacular upward 'blip' when thousands of returning World War II servicemen found all was not sweetness and light on the home front.

By 1993, the number of divorces had hit a record 165,000, with 176,000 children involved. Last year the divorce total dropped by 10,000, a move hailed by experts at Relate, formerly the Marriage Guidance Council, as evidence that more couples are realising the traumatic effects that break-ups have on children.

But there could be a quite different reason – the number of people getting married in the first place is tailing off significantly.

© *The Daily Mail*
November, 1995

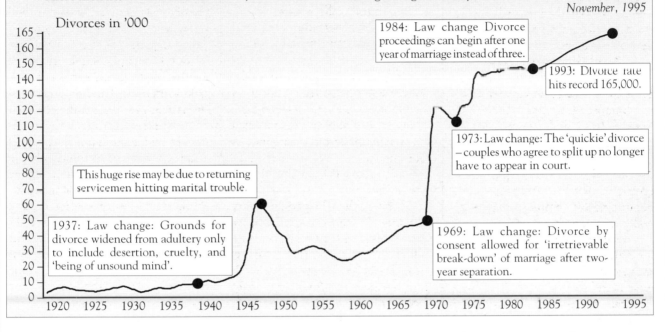

Divorces in '000

1984: Law change Divorce proceedings can begin after one year of marriage instead of three.

1993: Divorce rate hits record 165,000.

1973: Law change: The 'quickie' divorce – couples who agree to split up no longer have to appear in court.

This huge rise may be due to returning servicemen hitting marital trouble.

1937: Law change: Grounds for divorce widened from adultery only to include desertion, cruelty, and 'being of unsound mind'.

1969: Law change: Divorce by consent allowed for 'irretrievable break-down' of marriage after two-year separation.

The way Europe splits

Rules on divorce around Europe

France
Mutual consent after six months; automatic divorce after six years' separation; 'fault' divorce at any time on the grounds of adultery, unacceptable behaviour etc.

Spain
Divorce after two years' separation with consent, or five years' without. Legal separation on grounds of adultery, cruelty or desertion, or if the marriage has lasted at least a year.

Germany
If mutual agreement, automatic after one year's separation. If contested, courts can insist on up to five-year waiting period.

Britain
No proceedings can start until a year after marriage. Divorce available within three to six months on grounds of adultery or unreasonable behaviour. Otherwise, after two years on grounds of desertion or separation with consent, or five years' separation without consent.

Sweden
Automatic divorce with no time stipulation if parties agree and there are no children under 16. Otherwise, a six-month deliberation period.

Finland
On demand assuming consent and no young children. With children, six-month period of reflection or two years' formal separation required.

Italy
Divorce after legal separation for three years

Russia
Automatic after three months if parties agree, no young children or property involved. Otherwise couples must go to court.

Ireland
No-fault divorce for couples living apart for four out of preceding five years.
© *The Guardian*

A divorce history

AD950: Under the laws of Hywell Dda, ruler of Wales, provision is made for property to be divided fairly between partners after divorce.

1533: Pope Clement VIII refuses to annul the marriage of Henry VIII to Catherine of Aragon so that he can marry Anne Boleyn.

1534: The English parliament is compelled by Henry VIII to pass acts separating the English Church from Rome and make him its head. The principle of ecclesiastical divorce is established: there must be proof that the original marriage contract is invalid, meaning that in the eyes of the Church the marriage has never taken place.

1546: The first civil, as opposed to ecclesiastical, divorce, granted by a special Act of Parliament in order to make lawful the bigamous marriage of Lady Sadleir of Standon in Hertfordshire.

1551: The first civil divorce on the grounds of adultery, granted to the Marquess of Northampton, since described as 'the first real inroad on the indissolubility of Christian matrimony'.

1857: Divorce courts, established under the Matrimonial Causes Act, enable the middle classes to divorce in numbers.

1937: Matrimonial Causes Bill is passed in the House of Lords extending the grounds for both divorce and nullity proceedings, and prohibits divorce for three years after marriage, except in cases of special hardship. Grounds for divorce are: adultery, desertion for three years, cruelty, incurable insanity of five years'

standing, and unnatural offences by the husband.

1939: The British Privy Council accepts the Muslim practice of instant divorce, whereby a husband can divorce his wife by simply saying *Talaq* ('I divorce thee') three times in a row.

1949: Legal aid is introduced for divorcing couples, making divorce possible for all classes.

1965: The updated Matrimonial Causes Act enlarges the categories in the 1937 Bill, including changing 'unnatural offences' to rape, sodomy or bestiality.

1969: The Divorce Reform Act, a major breakthrough in divorce legislation, takes away the issue of 'guilt'. Courts now have to be satisfied that the marriage has 'irretrievably broken down'. Thus ends the practice of husbands popping down to a Brighton hotel with a prostitute and a camera to get proof in court of adultery

1970: The first case of 'palimony', a term credited to lawyer Marvin

Mitchelson, whose client, Michelle Triola, unsuccessfully sued Hollywood star Lee Marvin in California for half of his property. In the UK, live-in partners enjoy few rights.

1989: Under the Children's Act, if a woman remarries, maintenance ceases to be paid to her but financial provision for the children must continue.

1992: Dubbed 'gal-imony' by the tabloids, Judy Nelson takes Martina Navratilova to court, arguing that she deserves half of Navratilova's wealth as her partner for seven years. In court, Nelson provides a video tape of her and Navratilova 'solemnising' their relationship. Nelson walks away with their luxury home in Aspen, Colorado, and a cash settlement of $1 million. Same-sex marriage is not allowed in the UK.

1993: A statistical high: 165,000 British couples divorce, 350,000 get married.

1994: The Marriage Act allows civil weddings in any premises open to the public and approved by a local authority

1995: Lord Mackay's white paper removes the need to prove 'fault' in a marriage, such as adultery, unreasonable behaviour or desertion, but compels couples to spend a year in mediation and encourages them to negotiate their own settlements, thus greatly reducing the role of lawyers. The Government now proposes that England and Wales follow Scotland and require courts to take pension rights into account when splitting assets. © *The Independent January, 1996*

18

Myths and facts of 1990s divorce

From Families Need Fathers

Myth: Divorce is mainly caused by deserting husbands who walk away from their family responsibilities.

Fact: Only the smallest minority of divorces arise from desertion. Over three-quarters of divorce petitions are instigated by wives. The majority of these petitions are based upon the discredited grounds of 'unreasonable behaviour'. This type of petition is used where there is unilateral demand for a divorce but no acknowledged reason.

There is no requirement for any of the allegations of behaviour to be factual for divorce courts do not consider the concept of perjury to be valid. A husband is usually advised by his solicitor not to challenge or defend against such a petition, however false the contents, as resisting a divorce is a very expensive business and most lower courts take just the lodging of such a petition as legally recognised evidence of the 'irretrievable breakdown of marriage'.

Myth: Divorce is too easy / too difficult.

Fact: Divorce is neither of these. It is exactly as easy or as difficult as the parties make it. Where two people agree on the desirability of parting and are prepared to co-operate in giving proper support to their children (if any) divorce can go through with great ease.

If, however, a couple do not agree upon the wisdom of pursuing divorce or are unable to agree about the post-separation arrangements, divorce can become very extended and plagued with difficulties.

Myth: The acrimony in divorce is generated by the 'fault' base of our current law.

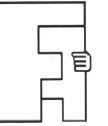

Fact: Few couples are directly concerned about the so-called marital-fault principles. A survey conducted in 1988 showed clearly that the main cause of bitterness in divorce arose from unjust arrangements regarding finances and contact with children. The only concern regarding 'fault' which arises is when false allegations are made in order to obtain financial benefit or to prejudice relationships with children of the marriage. This is a common practice.

Myth: In divorce matrimonial property and financial resources are divided equally between the parties.

Fact: Divorce courts have powers (which they invariably use) that are possessed by no other courts. The power to issue 'property-adjustment orders' gives total discretion to the court to divide property and finance without regard to the laws which pertain in the rest of society. The courts see it as their duty to give the much greater proportion of finance

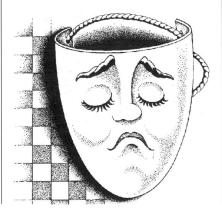

and property to a parent who obtains sole custody of children of the marriage. This is the main reason for so many divorcing wives seeking sole-custody orders in divorce even when sole custody is very obviously not in the best interests of the children. These property-adjustment orders can (and often do) lead to a father being rendered homeless by divorce even when the 'matrimonial home' had been purchased solely by him prior to marriage.

Myth: The children's rights of access to the non-resident parent are secured and enforced by court orders.

Fact: Court orders are certainly issued during divorce proceedings to protect children's rights of contact with the parent from whom they have been separated but, however blatantly they may be flouted by a resident parent, it is almost unheard of for there to be any enforcement by the courts. An application by a non-resident parent for enforcement of such an order can lead to a court withdrawing the children's rights of access altogether rather than upholding its previous decision.

Myth: The majority of single-parent mothers are reduced to poverty by divorce.

Fact: Where poverty has existed in the marriage, divorce will obviously make it worse. In most other cases a divorced mother will actually benefit financially from divorce by receiving maximum advantage under property-adjustment and maintenance orders. By contrast, most non-custodial fathers find themselves caught in the poverty-trap of homelessness and commitments to large sums of maintenance.

© Families Need Fathers

Can anyone be grown-up about this?

The news that your parents are divorcing can be devastating – even if you are an adult. Anna Moore reports

The impact of divorce on young children is well documented and seems to range from bed-wetting to hyperactivity to juvenile delinquency. Which is why some couples opt instead to stay together until their last child has grown up and gone. The divorce rate is rising across the board, and in 1993 more than 30,000 divorces occurred in marriages of more than 20 years.

But how does marital breakdown affect grown-up children? On the one hand, there is the expectation to act 'the grown-up' and 'cope', while at the same time watching what has built up through a lifetime suddenly disintegrate. One study has found that people whose parents divorce between the ages of 16 to 26 are five times more likely to develop psychiatric illness.

Gill Gorell Barnes, family therapist with the Tavistock Clinic, has counselled many adults who have experienced this. 'The biggest difference is the sudden, crushing sense of insecurity,' she says. 'People can't believe that what they grew up with has been wiped away.

'On the more positive side, it can sometimes force you to stop seeing them both as a blob called "parents" and instead forge entirely new adult relationships with each of them. Some people see their parents blooming and becoming interesting, feisty people in their own right – though, I must say, it's usually the mothers rather than the fathers.'

Denise Knowles at Relate says that late parental divorce can affect people's abilities to form their own relationships. 'It's a vulnerable time for someone who's just starting out, and it forces you to question absolutely everything. You feel that if this can happen to your parents after all that time, then nothing is certain.'

Brad was 23 when his father left their home in New Zealand for another woman. Now 31, he teaches in London.

Remembering the moment still makes me shiver. I was about to leave work when my phone rang. It was Mum, and she was hysterical, just screaming. 'He's left me. He's left me. Your father's left me.' I didn't know what she was talking about. I thought he'd gone for a walk or something. Then she said, 'There's a note. "Give my love to the kids".'

How does marital breakdown affect grown-up children?

It took an hour to drive to the family home – the house I'd grown up in and that Dad had built – and I was shaking all the way. My life passed before my eyes. My parents never rowed. We'd had the typical suburban scene – a son, a daughter, a dog, a beach house where we spent summers. I'd never considered that my parents wouldn't always be together.

When I got home, it was like he'd died. His cupboards were full of clothes, his garage was full of tools, he'd left everything behind. Just walked out on 27 years of life.

We learnt from the airport that he'd flown to England on that same day, and for eight months we heard nothing. As an adult, I had to cope and support my mother, but, as their child, I was traumatised. Overnight, I'd lost my family unit, and there was this huge feeling of failure. I'd thought we were happy – but how could we have been? I was also old enough to feel the stigma. Suddenly we were a soap opera come true.

Eventually, Dad started to write, and explain. Shortly before it happened, he'd gone to England to visit his mother and met another woman. The day he left us, she was waiting at Heathrow with a bottle of champagne. He says he was going through a breakdown, and had even considered suicide. Maybe when my sister and I had left home, he'd had to think hard about his relationship with Mum. They had married young, and he made me realise that my parents are humans, with separate emotions and pains – not just a unit.

The strongest feeling has been the vulnerability. I don't want anyone to get close to me because if someone can do that after 27 years, they can do anything. I didn't have a proper relationship for six years, and I'm still cynical about love and togetherness.

It's also left me without a 'home'. Both parents have remarried, and I've never lived with either of their new partners. So there's nowhere in the world where I can go back to, and completely belong, which partly explains why I've been travelling for six years.

My whole history – everything that created me – vanished on that day. I know I'm big enough to look after myself, but, unbelievably, eight years on, the loss can still almost make me cry.

Holly, 32, was 18 and about to leave home when her mother told her that she wished to separate from her father.

My parents seemed to have a good, strong relationship. I only remember hearing them argue once. I was close to both of them, and assumed they'd always be together. Now I see that Mum had been growing apart, but, because there were no blazing rows, we never noticed it. In a way I'm glad I kept hold of the illusion for so long.

Mum had married Dad when she was 18, and it had been very traditional, with Dad working as an engineer, and Mum in secretarial jobs. When I was 12, she got a job in a housing co-operative with lots of educated, middle-class people, and it was like a gradual awakening. She realised there were things she'd missed out on – she became more stroppy about her lack of help around the house. At the same time, Dad was forced to take jobs abroad.

It happened when he was in Barbados and Mum was flying out to visit the next day. She was lying in the bath, and just said, 'Tomorrow, I want to speak to Dad about separating.'

I remember feeling a really deep, deep sadness but making a conscious decision not to cry – that I was old enough to deal with it in a mature way. Mum had brought me and my sister up to be independent, career-oriented women, so I could rationally understand her decision. But emotionally, I still saw Dad as the victim. When I went out to visit him, it was very distressing because he couldn't accept it at all. At that point, there was a real role-reversal, as I worried about him and tried very gently to explain.

I never reproached Mum, but I suppose the resentment came out in other ways. In the months before I went to university, the two of us had to leave the house and move into a small flat, and we fought all the time. This was her bid for independence, and she still had a daughter round her neck. For me, there was a childish feeling that she was supposed to be my Mum, not some groovy feminist.

It's taken time, but Dad's been amazing. There's been no acrimony. Mum opened a restaurant, Dad came back to England, got a job, a flat, and 13 years on, they've settled into this really sweet friendship. I've learnt to see my parents as two individuals, and I'm proud of them. Neither has remarried, so my sister and I are still at the centre of their lives.

It's left me with a very realistic – or cynical – outlook on lifelong partnership, though. It's a tall order to expect to stay with someone for ever. I've seen how much people can

change over the years, and if the relationship can't accommodate those changes, it doesn't stand a chance.

Louise, 27, was at university when her parents split up after 33 years of marriage.

When I was 16, someone described us as the Kellogg's Cornflake family because we were sickeningly stable and happy. We'd always lived in the same house in the country. Dad phoned Mum from work every day, and arrived home at seven each evening. It was all you'd expect in an advert – and it hadn't changed in 20 years.

As the youngest, I was the last to leave. It was my second year at university when Mum phoned in tears to say that Dad had 'met someone else'.

It was impossible to take in – if she'd said he'd dropped dead, it would have at least been believable.

I felt basic, abject terror as my secure world disintegrated. For the next few days, as I lay in bed and cried, I also remember wondering what my university friends thought. Some had been through all this years before and 'got over it'. Was I childish, still needing my parents together when I'd left home anyway?

It seemed like a classic mid-life crisis. The kids had left, things were winding down, then Dad met someone he could start again with. My brothers and I all went home and rallied round. It was like a mourning for our shared history, really.

Not surprisingly, Dad found it harder to leave than he expected, and for the next six years he came back and forth, turning up in tears,

with Mum taking him back. Finally, they wore each other out and she told him to leave for good. They haven't spoken for over a year.

The unbelievable thing is that I have still never talked about this to Dad. During the times when we were both back home, we acted out the old routines as if nothing had happened. Now we both live in London we meet regularly and talk about absolutely anything except the fact that he has left Mum. I don't even know if he's living with this other woman – I never go to his flat and only contact him at work.

I still love him, but after 20 years of living within clear, safe roles, it's become too late and difficult to change them. There's also a lot of hurt that's probably best left repressed. I have an occasional dream where I finally confront this 'other woman' – whoever she is – and scratch her face off. It always wakes me crying.

Mum, on the other hand, has made a complete recovery. She's transformed from the traditional wife to someone who's utterly in charge. She has stayed in the family home, only now she runs it. She practically runs the village, actually, and has a far better social life than me. We're much closer than we'd have been otherwise, and we've done things like back-packing round India together.

Watching her bloom has been the most inspiring experience of my life. I truly believe that if she can cope with that, I should cope with just about anything.

© *The Independent December, 1995*

How children are damaged by divorce

When parents split up, they leave lasting emotional scars on their children. Ian Robertson reports

What happens to your children if you or your partner dies? It's the kind of thought which goes through the minds of most parents now and again. As a parent you have probably taken out life insurance with such a possibility in mind. From time to time you have worried about the effect on your child – emotionally, socially and financially – of losing you or your spouse. You know that children above a certain age never forget the death of a mother or father, and you appreciate that this may affect them for the rest of their lives.

But have you thought about what will happen to your children if you divorce or separate? You won't have taken out any insurance against this and you probably haven't thought about it as much as you have about the possibility of dying. This is a pity, because children are damaged much more by divorce than they are by parental death.

As many as one in three children in Britain will endure the consequences of parental divorce or separation; you can't get precise figures because almost a third of children are now born outside marriage and split-ups in these families are not officially recorded. If it is indeed true that boys and girls whose parents split up on average suffer more permanent damage than those whose mother or father dies, then this makes family breakdown one of the great unrecognised social health problems of our time. What is the evidence?

Dr Martin Richards, who runs the Centre for Family Research at Cambridge University, is an expert on divorce. He and his colleagues have studied 17,000 children from the National Child Development Survey who were born in Britain during one week in 1958 and were followed up at the ages of 7, 11, 16 and 23.

Dr Richards and his team looked at what happened to these children as they matured into adolescence and adulthood, comparing the ones whose mother or father had died with those whose parents had split up, in terms of education, career, health and wealth.

As many as one in three children in Britain will endure the consequences of parental divorce or separation

---

Although the harmful effects of divorce are apparent across all social classes, the effects on middle-class children are striking: middle-class girls were the group most damaged by divorce by the time they reached adulthood.

While the death of a mother or father before a child is 16 does have some effect on a child's life, divorce does far more damage. And if we examine, on average, the fortunes of young adults whose middle-class parents have divorced, compared with those whose parents have stayed together, the conclusions are stark. Children born of middle-class parents in 1958, who were not 16 before their parents divorced . . .

- had twice the chance of leaving school without any qualifications (boys and girls)
- had two-thirds the chance of going to university (boys and girls)
- were a third more likely not to have a full-time job at age 23 (boys)
- were two-thirds more likely not to have a full-time job at age 23 (girls)
- were four times more likely to be living in a council house at age 23 (boys and girls)
- were two-thirds more likely to be a regular smoker at age 23 (boys)

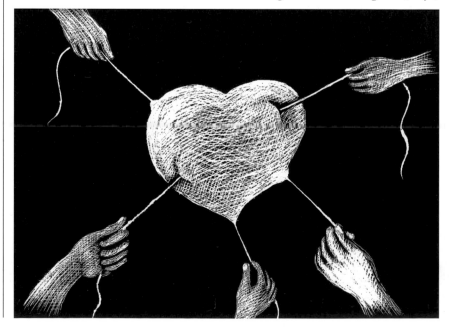

- were a third more likely to be a regular smoker at age 23 (girls)

Taking children of middle and working-class parents together, children of divorced parents were:

- twice as likely to have a child before age 20.
- twice as likely to be married or living with someone before age 20.

Dr Richards' research also found that children whose parents had divorced were on average less emotionally stable, left home earlier, and divorced or separated more frequently. They showed more behavioural problems in school, were more likely to be unhappy and worried, and were poorer at reading and arithmetic.

At the Cavendish Laboratory, Cambridge, where Rutherford once split the atom, Dr Richards and his colleagues now study the splitting of families. 'Low self-esteem may underlie a lot of these effects,' he says. 'Death of a parent doesn't produce the same problems. The critical thing seems to be children's awareness that parents have, through choice, separated, and for many this means a parent choosing to leave them.'

The resulting sense of abandonment, Dr Richards says, can haunt children into adulthood, leading them to undervalue their own worth, lack self-confidence and hence enter too rapidly into serious yet potentially vulnerable relationships at an early age.

'As a university teacher I see that even when children have left home and are in their early twenties, their parents' separation or divorce can be very disturbing for them. Adolescents are particularly vulnerable, probably for similar reasons; at a point when they are learning about relationships, they see the most important relationship in their lives fall apart.'

The differences between those whose parents have and have not divorced are most striking in young adult women from middle-class families. One reason for this may be that these women tend to embark on serious partnerships at an early age – perhaps seeking the emotional

Divorce and middle-class children

%	Boys			Girls		
	Parents together	Parent died	Parents divorced	Parents together	Parent died	Parents divorced
Left school at 16	48	52	75	47	55	77
Not in full time work	18	18	24	32	32	55
Living in council house	4	8	18	4	11	18
Regular smokers	36	29	58	32	36	42

and how further education suffers

%	Parents together	Parent died	Parents divorced
Go to University	31	27	19
Age 23 no qualifications	11	14	19

security and stability which their parents' divorce has denied them. As a result of having children so early, these middle-class young women miss the chance of going to university, and with that the career, income and fulfillment which they might have expected.

But the negative effects of divorce are not confined to young middle-class women – no class or gender is spared. Children whose parents have divorced are more likely to show symptoms of being unhappy and worried than children from intact families: for instance, divorced mothers more often report that their child worries about many things; is upset by new situations; is bullied by other children; is miserable or tearful; prefers to do things alone. This is true both at age seven and at age 16.

Children of divorced parents also tend to misbehave more than those from intact families, again at both ages. They are more likely to be rated by their mothers as: being disobedient at home; fighting with other children; being irritable and quick to fly off the handle; destroying others' belongings; being squirmy or fidgety; having difficulty settling to anything.

The majority of children of divorced parents end up living with their mothers, but if their mothers remarry the children tend to show more problems than those whose mothers stay single. 'Particularly for adolescents, it is very difficult to come to terms with a parent dating again,' Dr Richards says. He argues that good and regular contact with the absent father can reduce some of the ill-effects of separation, even though this may be at the expense of increased conflict between the parents: the sad fact, however, is that a half of all divorced fathers lose contact with their children within two years.

Dr Richards, 55, is himself a divorcé: 'I was 21 when I married, but we were too young and it didn't last. We had no children.' And now? 'I have grown-up children but have never remarried.' Divorce and family conflict can blight the lives of children – though it is important to remember that all the statistics available are average effects, and clearly there are many children who fare well when their parents separate. Furthermore, until the present generation of children has grown up, we will not know whether the effects of divorce will be as bad as they were for the children of 1958.

Children survive best where good contact is maintained with both parents. 'Many children learn that their parents are separating from a third party. Parents often do not talk to them and ask them what they want.'

And what do they want? Dr Richards pauses for a second. 'They almost always say they only want one thing,' he replies. 'That their parents should stay together.'

● Ian Robertson is a senior scientist at the MRC Applied Psychology Unit in Cambridge.

© Times Newspapers Ltd
May 1995

Wedded to divorce

How our neighbours break up

By Scott Hughes

Germany

A divorce can be granted by local courts on the overall grounds of 'breakdown', which will be assumed where matrimonial cohabitation has ended and cannot be expected to be resumed. Divorce may be pronounced, if it is sought by both spouses, after they have lived apart for a year, and if one refuses to resume cohabitation after three years. However, a divorce may be obtained within the first year of separation if the petitioner cannot reasonably be expected to remain within the marriage, and if the grounds invoked by the petitioner are connected with the personal behaviour of the other partner.

Denmark

A divorce can be granted after a year's legal separation, after six months' separation if the parties have agreed to divorce, after two years' living apart, or on the grounds of adultery, bigamy or gross ill-treatment of the other spouse or children. Most divorces are preceded by a legal separation. A divorce can be granted either by the courts or, under an administrative procedure, by the county governor. Divorces can usually be granted by the governor within one month and by the courts within two. Legal representation is not necessary in many cases, and the judge has no obligation to seek reconciliation or mediation before approving the divorce. There are about 32,000 marriages each year and 13,000 divorces out of a population of 5.2 million.

France

There are three main grounds for divorce: divorce by mutual consent, divorce based on the fault of one of the partners (for instance adultery, or a criminal conviction) and divorce after separation where the spouses have lived apart for a continuous period of at least six years. The average length of proceedings is about eight and a half months where there is agreement and 10 months where there is no agreement. Divorce proceedings based on separation take 15 months. The divorce judge is the family judge in the area where the matrimonial home is located.

The family judge must discuss the possibility of reconciliation. Even if the reconciliation is not successful, the judge cannot announce the divorce immediately because there has to be a three-month waiting period.

Italy

Divorce terminates civil marriages, but the Catholic Church does not recognise divorce. A joint petition for divorce takes about four months

to process. A spouse can petition for divorce on these grounds: after three years' separation, where one partner has committed serious crimes, when the marriage has not been consummated, where a party is transsexual, or when a foreign annulment of the marriage has been obtained. The judge must attempt a reconciliation and can refuse to accept the divorce even if grounds for a breakdown can be established, although this rarely happens. The parties have a 30-day period to reflect on their decision or allow time for appeal before the court's decision is officially registered.

Netherlands

In 1993, there were 88,000 marriages and 30,000 divorces in a population of 15m. In 1960, there were only 6,000 divorces. The only grounds for divorce is that the marriage has irretrievably broken down. This can be proven by a joint petition or by the continued assertion of the breakdown by one of the parties. The petitioner only need maintain the belief that the marriage has broken down throughout the proceedings to prove grounds for divorce, even if the breakdown is contested. Cases determined by separation are rare.

Switzerland

The most common ground for divorce is irretrievable breakdown. Judges make orders regarding the terms of divorce. In the canton of Zurich, as well as other cantons, divorce proceedings cannot be started unless the parties first apply for mediation with a justice of the peace. In 1992, there were 45,080 marriages and 14,530 divorces.

(Source: *Family Law in Europe*, edited by Carolyn Hamilton and Kate Standley, Butterworth.)

Deeds of Separation

From Families need Fathers

However distressing a separation may be, it can usually be made worse by a battle in the courts. Wherever possible a voluntary agreement is infinitely better. Fortunately, an increasing number of people are availing themselves of the Conciliation Services which are being set up around the country. And so more and more voluntary agreements are being made. The problem with such agreements is that they may not be legally binding.

A Deed of Separation may be the ideal solution to such a problem. They are particularly suitable where there is no immediate wish for a divorce. As one is rarely told by solicitors that such a document exists the following description of an actual Deed may be of interest. It outlines the issues that may be covered.

The first paragraph contains the names and addresses of the parties, the date of the marriage and the date of birth of the child. It also gives an introduction to legal jargon, e.g. ' . . . aforesaid his wife (herein called the wife) of the other part'!!

An important clause in this section states that the parties have had independent legal advice. This is not just for the benefit of the solicitors. It means that the Deed would be far more likely to stand up in court if it was contested. If one side could show that they signed it under duress while in an emotional state and without legal advice, it could well be nullified by a court.

The agreements are divided into four groups: The first of these groups contains important agreements on the future relationships between the members of the family. Of these the first is obvious: the husband and wife would live apart and not bother each other or their acquaintances in any way.

The second agreement in this group states that the parents would have joint custody and that the child would remain in the care and control of the wife. It also defines the access. (One would expect joint custody to be the norm in Deeds of Separation and access of up to 50%. There would probably have been joint care and control if the solicitor had been better informed. These concepts are of course being superseded by the Children Bill.)

The third agreement is an interesting one. It states that the husband and wife absolutely forgave and released any matrimonial offence or cause of complaint etc. In short, it entails that neither party could quote past actions in any future proceedings. Essentially it is a commitment to make the Deed work. The last agreement in this group commits each party to consent to a divorce if the other petitions for one on the grounds that the marriage had irretrievably broken down after two years.

The second group of agreements contains the husband's covenants. In this case the settlement was a lump sum 'in full and final settlement'. A second paragraph states that he would deliver to his wife some specified items which were hers.

The next group lists the wife's covenants. These include the transfer of her share of those hallmarks of middle-class life. The house, the bank account and the car. A notable paragraph in this section contains the agreement that she would at all times support and maintain herself and support and maintain the child when the child was living with her. The agreement on the child's maintenance would not, of course, have any standing in law, as a person cannot sign away the rights of a third party. In this case, the father would have the child about half the time, and as such bear half the child's expenses. The other half would be partly covered by the capital payment. The form of the agreement may have important tax implications and professional advice should be sought. The final agreement in this section is that the wife would not claim further financial provision in any subsequent divorce or other proceedings.

The last group contains a number of sundry agreements, such as that the parties would not claim any inheritances if the other died and that each would bear the legal costs of preparing the deed etc.

It is hoped that this thumbnail sketch of a signed Deed of Separation containing voluntary agreements may be of help to those who feel that they have had enough blood-letting and wish to avoid the damage of an acrimonious court hearing, where nobody seems to win except the solicitors. At the end of the day, the strength of a Deed depends on how it would stand up in court if challenged. A well-drafted agreement that is eminently fair would have little difficulty in this respect.

The main value of a Deed of Separation is that it contributes to the goodwill between parents, which is essential for the children's well-being. The working of the Deed described makes this clear. This is the opposite to court action, which seems to compound the adversarial elements of the relationship, which is never in the children's interests.

● The above is an extract from an information sheet produced by Families need Fathers. See page 39 for address details.

Mediation eased the pain

When Chris and Naomi Schrecker decided to divorce they felt they had lost everything. Their seven-year marriage was dead and their young sons were caught in the crossfire. Only a visit to their local Family Mediation Service restored their faith in the future

By Clare Garner

Mrs Schrecker, 40, was suspicious of any outside interference in her marriage break-up. Her husband had moved out and there was no question of a reconciliation. Reluctantly, she agreed to go with him to the centre in Bury, Lancashire, and, four years on, both partners are thankful they did so.

'We couldn't make decisions together or discuss anything. We couldn't communicate and it was frightening for the children,' said Mrs Schrecker, a schoolteacher.

'I was very wary of going to mediation. I was on my guard and very defensive. I felt emotionally disabled when I got into that room and worried that they would get me to agree to all sorts of things that would prolong the pain.'

Instead, like her husband, she found that the counsellors took the heat out of the situation. They attended a joint session once a month and slowly it became possible for them to make plans in the short term. Arrangements like Christmas and the holidays, as well as more mundane day-to-day matters, were always discussed within the confines of the centre.

'It made all the difference in the world,' said Mrs Schrecker. 'They were very patient and dealt with us very tactfully. Slowly our relationship settled down to what it is now. It's quite formal but we do support each other, particularly professionally. I now have a productive, happy life and hope that in the future we can bring up our children in a way that brings the best out of both of us.'

Mr Schrecker, 38, contacted the Family Mediation Service in 1991 because he was worried about the children.

'What I was looking for at that stage was a way of actually coming to some sort of practical agreement over the children being able to see both of us in a reasonably confrontation-free atmosphere,' he said.

At the time, his two sons, now aged four and 11, were living with their mother in the family home in Prestwich, Manchester, and he was visiting them for a brief, tense period each day.

'It was a difficult sort of arrangement. It was very stressful because a lot of feelings of anger and betrayal tended to manifest themselves at the times when we handed over the children,' said Mr Schrecker, also a schoolteacher.

The Family Mediation Service, managed by the nation-wide charity NCH Action for Children, enabled the couple to air their disputes in a safe environment.

'The bitterness was moved to an arena where it was properly dealt with rather than being spontaneous outbreaks,' said Mr Schrecker.

'The service helped each of us step by step to build a relationship with the children which allows for the other's presence.'

Their divorce papers came through in June this year. The children now spend three days and two nights a week with their father and the rest of the time with their mother, a situation with which both parents are happy.

'Under the terms of the Children's Act the courts do now allow, thank God, for parties to come to their own arrangements over children,' said Mr Schrecker.

'Unfortunately, I believe the service exists only in certain parts of the country,' he added. 'We are very lucky to have had the service in the area.'

© *The Independent*
October, 1995

32

What happens to me when my parents split up?

Information for children and young people

What splitting up means to you

Your parents will always be your Mum and Dad whatever happens. Parents do not always get on together. Even when they both care a lot for you, they may not be able to live together. Splitting up and divorce happens quite often now and you will probably know someone whose parents have split up. Try asking them how they got on and what happened to them.

Feelings

You may feel angry, confused or frightened. You might be relieved about some things and sad about others.

You may have all of these feelings at the same time which is really confusing. The good news is that feeling bad does not last forever.

Getting help

Talking does help. You may be able to talk to your parents and get some answers to the questions that are bothering you. If your parents find it difficult to discuss what is happening with you, think about a grown-up whom you could talk to . . .maybe a teacher or youth-club leader.

Grown-ups don't always find it easy to start talking about important things, but if you ask questions, and let them know you need to talk, they will usually try to help.

Parents' feelings

Your parents will have all sorts of jumbled-up feelings about the split-up. They may be too angry, confused or tired to take time to explain to you what is happening, or to do the usual things with you. They may not understand how you can love your other parent. Things usually get better as time goes on. There are people around who can help your parents sort out their problems.

Deciding where you live

Very often parents decide between them who is best able to look after the children. Sometimes both would like to look after you, but only one can. Your parents may ask for your ideas. Perhaps you are feeling confused just now, and if you are not sure whom you want to live with, it may help to talk to another grown-up, apart from your parents, about it. This person could help to explain your feelings to your parents.

Sometimes your parents cannot agree whom you should live with, and then a judge at court will have to decide what happens.

If you do not want to visit your other parent, your wishes should be considered. Talk over any problems like these or your feelings with your parents or a trusted adult.

If visits are not arranged at the time your parents split up and you lose contact with the parent who has left, you may want to get in touch later. Discuss this with the parent you live with or an adult that you can trust.

Maybe your other parent has moved away, or doesn't know that it's important to you to see him or her. It might be possible to write, send photographs, phone, or simply keep your parent's address. In future, you might be able to get in touch with your parent again.

New partners

Sometimes one or both parents may find a new partner. This can make you feel strange because the new partner may seem to be taking the place of your other parent. You may feel angry, jealous and pushed out by the new person or you may like them from the beginning. The grown-ups can also feel awkward at the beginning of a new relationship. Sometimes the parent you live with will get a new partner who may also have children. This may mean getting to know them and perhaps living together as a new family which can be difficult. Talking about how you feel, and finding out the new 'rules' in the home, can help to make life easier for everyone. If the parent you don't live with has a new partner, there is no reason to stop visiting just because there is someone else around.

Some words you will hear

Separation: This is the time when a couple are living apart but may not have decided to make this permanent.

Divorce: When a married couple decide to split up, a judge at court has to grant them a divorce to end their marriage.

Care and control: This is the day-to-day responsibility for looking after and making everyday decisions about a child. The parent who has care and control is the person you live with for most of the time.

Access: Seeing the parent you don't live with is called 'access'.

Custody: This is a legal word which means the right to make important decisions for a child, about things like education, medical treatment and religion. It may also involve permission to travel abroad or consent to marry. This right may be shared by both parents, who will continue to make important decisions together for their child. This is called joint custody. When the right is given to one parent only, who usually has care and control too, it is called sole custody. (In practice, both parents often discuss important decisions even when one parent has sole custody.)

© Northern Ireland Family Mediation Service

Guidelines for separating parents

Guidelines for contact

The child's adjustment to his or her parents' divorce will be greatly enhanced if the parents can establish a schedule for contact in a positive and co-operative manner. The following guidelines can assist divorcing parents in avoiding common problems.

1. The parent with whom the child lives should make every effort to reassure the child that he/she approves of the child's contact with the other parent. The parent should actively encourage the child to attend and enjoy visits

2. The visiting parent should ensure that the other parent knows the general whereabouts of the children, and has a contact telephone number when the children are away on extended visits.

3. Disagreements about suitability of clothing or visits should be discussed between parents, not with the children.

4. Every effort should be made by both parents to keep within time-scales which have been agreed.

5. Parents should respect each other's privacy and recognise that inter-rogating a child during or after visits may lessen the child's enjoyment of those visits.

6. Parents should avoid making negative comments about the other parent either to the child or in his or her presence

7. A child who acts withdrawn after a visit is not necessarily reflecting a contact problem, but rather reflecting his or her level of stress and concern regarding the changes in the family.

8. Parents should assume responsibility for arranging visits.

9. It is important for children, particularly younger children, to have a consistent and predictable schedule when they can anticipate seeing their absent parent.

Information from Families Need Fathers

10. Periods of extended contact allow the parent-child relationship to develop in a more realistic manner.

11. Contact between children and their absent parents occurs more smoothly and therefore more beneficially for the children when the parents are able to communicate and encourage positive feelings about each other.

Keeping contact

For the great majority of children there is no doubt that their interests will be best served by efforts to sustain links with their natural families. Contact in the form of personal visits and meetings will generally be the most common and, for both parent and child, the most satisfactory way of maintaining their relationship

But other means which can help to keep family bonds alive should be borne in mind: letters, telephone calls, exchange of photographs.

Such contacts – however occasional – may continue to have value for the child even when other contact has ended. These contacts can keep alive for a child a sense of his or her origins and may keep open options for family relationships in later life.

The wider family

Consideration of contact should take into account the child's wider family, and should not overlook the problems which may arise when the parent with whom the child resides may be reluctant to provide such contact.

The child's wishes

Sometimes children are openly unwilling to see a parent, or have ambivalent feelings about contact. Unfortunately such children are unlikely to be able to appreciate the short – or long-term effects of a decision not to have contact – both on themselves and the other person. Carers must attempt to understand the source of these feelings and help the child understand them so that visits can become a source of enjoyment and advantage. Contact should not be allowed to lapse until after real efforts have been made to help the child understand what is likely to be of greatest benefit to him or her.

Choice of venue

Natural parents need help in seeing their child in someone else's home, living as part of someone else's family. Sometimes the visits to the children's home can be so stressful to one of the parties that tensions cannot be quickly resolved and help may be required to deal with the practical aspects of contact. Occasionally an alternative venue for meeting may have to be found.

The impact of divorce on adults

The assistance of an objective, trained counsellor has proved helpful to many people faced with the end of a relationship.

For some couples divorce may be a mutual decision, but for most the choice is made by one spouse, much to the disappointment of the other, leading to strong and uncomfortable emotions.

Frequently sadness gradually turns into anger as the need to find blame strengthens. Later, feelings of sadness and loss are acknowledged and the relationship 'let go'.

The impact of divorce on children

Children are particularly vulnerable and sensitive to the stresses of a divorce, but with thoughtful parenting they should be able to make a normal and healthy adjustment within a relatively short period of time

Children will generally experience a variety of feelings, normally:
- insecurity
- fear of abandonment
- depression
- sadness
- anger
- loneliness
- self-blame, guilt
- conflicting loyalties

These feelings may be acted out through troublesome behaviour:
- temper outbursts and aggressive behaviour
- reduction in school performance
- alignment with one parent
- reconciliation fantasies

Infants and toddlers – need to feel secure in their environment. Contact should be consistent, frequent and in an appropriate environment.

Pre-school children – have a sense of good and bad, and with this comes guilt. These children may blame themselves for the divorce. They are also vulnerable to perceptions of abandonment by a parent.

Pre-adolescents – are susceptible to emotional manipulation. They have a tendency to take sides and act out against the parent they perceive as blameworthy. This needs to be diffused and the child helped to work out his or her anger.

Adolescents – continue to have a need for parental guidance and guidelines, requiring the time, energy and participation of both parents.

The reactions described above are normal. It is important to recognise the need for assistance when a child's reaction is severe or prolonged.

Fortunately, however, most children quickly regain their balance. This is especially true when both parents are able to co-operate in fulfilling the task of commitment they started together, raising their children.

Guidelines for parents

Explanation of the divorce:
The children need to be provided with an explanation of the divorce, which may need to be re-explained as they grow older.

Feelings of guilt and blame:
Children need ongoing reassurance from their parents that the children were not responsible for the divorce.

Fear of rejection and abandonment:
Children need to be reassured of continued love from both parents by consistent contact through visits, phone calls etc.

Parental undermining/criticism:
Parents should avoid criticism of the other parent to the child or in the child's presence.

Parental communications:
Parents need to avoid placing the child in the unfair position of carrying messages between them regarding visits, finance etc.

Changing financial situation:
Parents should not unfairly burden the children with unnecessary details.

Consistency of parenting:
Parents should prepare a plan for consistent child-care which makes as few changes to the child's daily routine as possible.

Extended family members:
Parents should make efforts to maintain the children's contacts with their extended family.

Reconciliation fantasies:
Parents should be truthful and help the child to deal with the realities of the divorce from the outset.

© *Families Need Fathers*

Parenthood does not end when a partnership does

From the Network of Access and Child Contact Centres (NACCC)

What are Contact Centres?
They are neutral meeting-places where children of separated families can enjoy contact with one, or both, parents (and sometimes other family members) in a comfortable and safe environment where there is no viable alternative. Whilst children are at a Centre their parents maintain complete responsibility for them.

What is their aim?
To provide short-term help and support towards establishing meaningful contact between child and visiting parent.

Who are they run by?
Churches, Councils for Voluntary Service, WRVS, Court Welfare Service and voluntary groups. They will be staffed by three or four volunteers at each session, whose function is to make contact an enjoyable experience for the child and visiting parent.

Who makes referrals to Centres?
Most referrals are made by solicitors, court welfare officers or social workers.

Where are the Centres
There are now well over 150 Centres spread throughout the country. The Network of Access & Child Contact Centres (NACCC) produces an annual directory of all known Centres, listed in order of county, for which the cost is just £6.50. Monthly update lists are posted to purchasers of the directory on payment of an additional £12.00, to cover production and postage costs.

What about charges?
Virtually all Centres offer their services free of charge. Most provide light refreshments at a reasonable cost.

So what is NACCC?
The Network is a national federation of Access/Contact Centres, each operating independently, but subscribing to a Code of Practice.

NACCC has two main aims:
1. To promote the establishment of new Contact Centres.
2. To support existing Centres by sharing relevant information and training resources.

Why Centres join NACCC
NACCC acts on behalf of members at national level, corresponding with the Children's Act Advisory Committee and similar organisations. The Network also provides a forum for problem-sharing both regionally and nationally. Its handbook is a must for new or established Centres and *Network Live*, published three times a year, keeps members up to date with developments and changes in legislation as they affect our work. As well as the NACCC training

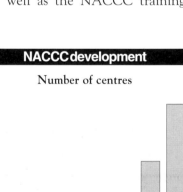

NACCC development

Number of centres

1988 1989 1990 1991 1992 1993 1994 1995

video, workshops on a wide range of contact-related matters are available to members at reduced rates.

If you would like further information about NACCC, or a copy of the directory and update lists, please write to:
The Administrator, NACCC
St Andrew's with Castle Gate
United Reformed Church
Goldsmith Street
Nottingham NG1 5JT

Cheques, made payable to NACCC, should be sent with any orders.

Code of Practice
1. Contact is child centred. Work with parents is aimed at making contact/access less stressful for the child.

2. Impartiality is fundamental to the operation of a Centre.

3. The Centre is not primarily a negotiating ground. Its purpose is to help parents put into practice agreements or arrangements made elsewhere.

4. The access/contact process requires an explicit policy about confidentiality. Everyone involved with a Centre must be informed of this policy.

5. Training and support for volunteers is essential.

6 Centres will seek to ensure that its volunteers are made aware of the particular needs of parents and children attending the Centre.

7. Centres exist within a multi-culture, multi-faith society and should seek to act in ways which reflect this.

© Network of Access and Child Contact Centres (NACCC) January, 1996

Divorce

Splits between individuals fissure society with 95,000 family breakdowns every year

By Sally Weale

When Charles and Diana finally oblige the Queen and untie the royal marital knot, they will join more than 155,000 couples whose marriages end in the divorce courts every year.

At one time, Prince Harry and Prince William, as children of divorced parents, might have been the exception in their school class. But not now. In 1993, 95,000 divorcing couples had children under 16.

A growing proportion of children are being affected by marital breakdown, though three out of 10 divorcing couples are childless with most divorces occurring between five and nine years of marriage.

In 1993, there were 176,000 children under 16 whose families were broken by divorce, and it is estimated that one in four of today's children will experience divorce before they reach 16.

In many ways Charles and Diana are simply conforming to a wider pattern of marital breakdown in society.

Having notched up 14 years of marriage, they have perhaps lasted longer than might be expected in a society in which 40 per cent of new unions are expected to end in divorce after an average of 9.8 years.

There are clear differences in their case, however. Whereas it is clearly Prince Charles who is pushing for a divorce, in general 70 per cent of petitions are filed by women.

And though in most cases each partner loses on average 40 per cent of their income as a result of divorce, neither Charles nor Diana are expected to lose out on that score.

Though statistics for the record number of marriage breakdowns within one family are not immediately available, the Royal Family must rate a mention in any future study. They make it look contagious.

Of the Queen's four children, one has already been divorced, a second seems about to follow suit and a third is separated, though enjoying something of a renaissance in his relationship with his estranged wife.

The fourth has taken the safe option thus far and avoided marriage, though now even Edward, despite his family's appalling record on marriage, seems about to take the plunge with Sophie Rhys-Jones.

Some research has suggested there is an element of inter-generational transmission of divorce – people whose parents are divorced are statistically more likely to divorce themselves, although divorce does not necessarily run in families. Indeed, Princess Diana made it clear in her *Panorama* interview that, having been brought up in a divorced family, she did not wish to inflict that experience on her own children.

Research has shown that children of divorce do worse in school, in work and in their own marriages, though whether it is the fact of divorce or simply a conflict between parents which is to blame is unclear.

At the end of the day it may be just as well that Prince Charles has declared his intention not to marry again, since the prognosis for second marriages is not good. In 1992, a third of all divorces was a second or third divorce for one or both partners.

And he might even rue the day he divorced Diana. One study of divorcees found that men live to regret it more than women. More than 50 per cent of divorced men said they would have preferred to stay married, compared with 29 per cent of women.

The Wales's should be warned that divorce is bad for health, with cancer rates significantly higher among the divorced population, and life expectancy among the married five years greater than that among the divorced.

A spokeswoman for the marriage research charity, One Plus One, said: 'Divorced people tend to have worse health. 'They smoke more, they drink more and they have higher rates of unsafe sex with more partners.'

© The Guardian
December, 1995

INDEX

ADDITIONAL RESOURCES

You might like to contact the following organisations for further information. Due to the increasing cost of postage, many organisations cannot respond to enquiries unless they receive a stamped, addressed envelope.

Barnardos
Tanners Lane
Barkingside
Ilford
Essex IG6 1QG
Tel: 0181 550 8822
Fax: 0181 551 6870
Works with families to help them enjoy a stable and caring family life. Produces publications.

Divorce Conciliation and Advisory Service (DCAS)
38 Ebury Street
London
SW1W 0LU
Tel: 0171 730 2422
Works to help parents to maintain workable arrangements for the joint care of their children after a divorce or separation.

Families Need Fathers
134 Curtain Road
London
EC2A 3AR
Tel: 0171 613 5060
Fax: 0171 613 5060
Families Need Fathers is primarily concerned with the problems of maintaining a child's relationship with both parents following separation and divorce. Produces publications.

Family and Youth Concern
322 Woodstock Road
Oxford OX2 7NS
Tel: 01865 568 48
Support of the family founded on marriage.

Family Mediation Scotland
127 Rose Street
South Lane
Edinburgh EH2 4BB
Tel: 0131 220 1610
Fax: 0131 220 6895
Acts as a co-ordinator for mediation services in Scotland. Produces leaflets for children, parents, teachers, solicitors and booklets for the general public.

Family Policy Studies Centre
231 Baker Street
London NW1 6XE
Tel: 0171 486 8211
Describes and analyses family trends and consider their implications for public policy; to consider the impact of policies on families of different kinds. They publish a wide range of materials including newsletters, bulletins and reports including *Families in the European Union*.

Institute of Family Therapy
43 New Cavendish Street
London
W1M 7RG
Tel: 0171 935 1651
Provide counselling for couples, mediation for couples and families, and training for family therapists.

National Children's Bureau
8 Wakely Street
London EC1V 7QE
Tel: 0171 843 6000
Fax: 0171 843 6000
Provides information on children's needs in the family, school and society. They publish a series on factsheets called *Highlights*.

NCH Action for Children
85 Highbury Park
London N5 1UD
Tel: 0171 226 2033
Fax: 0171 226 2537
Runs family and community centres nationwide for children and families.

Network of Access and Child Contact Centres (NACCC)
St Andrew's with Castlegate Church
Goldsmith Street
Nottingham NG1 5JT
Tel: 0115 948 4557
Works to relieve the emotional distress caused by the break-up of family relationships. Produces publications.

Northern Ireland Family Mediation Service
76 Dublin Road
Belfast
BT2 7HP
Tel: 01232 322914
Acts as a co-ordinator for mediation services throughout Northern Ireland. Produces leaflets for children, parents, teachers, solicitors and booklets for the general public.

One plus One Marriage and Partnership Research
12 New Burlington Street
London
W1X 1FF
Tel: 0171 734 2020
Fax: 0171 734 3857
Conducts research into the causes of marriage breakdown and divorce. They publish a useful information pack suitable for students and the general public.

Relate
Herbert Gray College
Little Church Street
Rugby
CV21 3AP
Tel: 01788 573241
Fax: 01788 535007
Co-ordinates about 130 local Relate centres which provide counselling for those with relationship problems. Selects and trains therapists and has a specialist bookshop. Produces publications.

The National Council for Family Proceedings
University of Bristol
3 Priory Road
Bristol
BS8 1TX
Tel: 0117 928 8136
Fax: 0117 974 1299
Provides conferences and training. Publishes newsletters, leaflets and other information on family proceedings.

ACKNOWLEDGEMENTS

The publisher is grateful for permission to reproduce the following material.

Chapter One: Marriage

Family crisis affects us all, © The Daily Express, August 1995, *Marriage goes on trial as its attraction wanes,* © The Telegraph plc, London 1995, *Marriage still children's goal,* © The Guardian, *Forward to basics,* © The Telegraph plc, London 1995, *Wrangle over cohabitation figures,* © The Guardian, December 1995, *The decline and rise of the family,* © Focus, January 1995, *Changes in family structure,* © Barnardos, *Making a success of marriage,* © Family Policy Studies Centre, November 1995, *Mum's no longer the word for many women,* © The Telegraph plc, London 1995, *Family index,* © Family Policy Studies Centre, November 1995, *A man for all reasons,* © The Guardian, September 1995, *44 pc of pregnancies now occur outside marriage,* © The Telegraph plc, London 1995.

Chapter Two: Divorce

Divorce rate falls after years of relentless rise, © The Telegraph plc, London 1995, *How every change has made breaking up easier to do,* © The Daily Mail, November 1995, *The way Europe splits,* © The Guardian, November 1995, *A divorce history,* © The Independent, *Myths and facts of 1990s divorce,* © Families need Fathers, *The map of divorce,* © The Daily Mail, December 1995, *Can we be grown-up about this?,* © The Independent, December 1995, *How children are damaged by divorce,* © The Times, May 1995, *I chose the man I wanted to father my baby,* © The Daily Mail, December 1995, *Wedded to divorce,* © The Independent, November 1995, *Deeds of Separation,* © Families need Fathers, 1995, *The Family Mediation Service,* © The Family Mediation Service, *Mediation eased the pain,* © The Independent, October 1995, *What happens to me when my parents split up?,* © People Projects, Bristol, and the Children's Society, London, *Guidelines for separating parents,* © Families need Fathers, *Parenthood does not end when a relationship does,* © Network of Child Contact Centres (NACCC), *Divorce,* © The Guardian, December 1995.

Photographs and Illustrations

Page 1: Andrew Smith / Folio Collective, pages 8, 10, 27, 32, 37: Ken Pyne, pages 12, 24: Katherine Fleming / Folio Collective, pages 14, 23: Anthony Haythornthwaite / Folio Collective, page 31: Graphic News.

Craig Donnellan
Cambridge
April, 1996